Israel in Bible Prophecy

Past, Present & Future

Dr. David R. Reagan

www.lamblion.com

Dedicated to

Joel Chernoff
General Secretary
of the Messianic Jewish Alliance of America
A legendary Messianic musician
and a visionary Messianic leader

First edition, 2017
Second Printing, 2018

ISBN: 978-0-945593-28-7

Library of Congress Control Number: 2017901218

Lamb & Lion Ministries
P.O. Box 919
McKinney, Texas 75070
lamblion@lamblion.com
www.lamblion.com

The cover painting, "Jews at the Wailing Wall"
is by Gustav Bauernfeind (1848-1904).

Cover design by Trey Collich.

Printed in the United States of America.

Contents

Part 3: The Future

(All maps by Stephen Cymerman: stephen@cymerman.com.)

Deuteronomy 4:27-31

27) "The LORD will scatter you among the peoples, and you will be left few in number among the nations where the LORD drives you.

28) "There you will serve gods, the work of man's hands, wood and stone, which neither see nor hear nor eat nor smell.

29) "But from there you will seek the LORD your God, and you will find Him if you search for Him with all your heart and all your soul.

30) "When you are in distress and all these things have come upon you, in the latter days you will return to the LORD your God and listen to His voice.

31) "For the LORD your God is a compassionate God; He will not fail you nor destroy you nor forget the covenant with your fathers which He swore to them."

Books by Dr. David R. Reagan

The Christ in Prophecy Study Guide (McKinney, TX: Lamb & Lion Ministries, 1987). Second edition in 2001. Third edition in 2006.

Trusting God: Learning to Walk by Faith (Lafayette, LA: Huntington House, 1987). Second edition in 1994. Third edition in 2015.

Jesus is Coming Again! (Eugene, OR: Harvest House, 1992). Second edition in 2015.

The Master Plan: Making Sense of the Controversies Surrounding Bible Prophecy Today (Eugene, OR: Harvest House, 1993).

Living for Christ in the End Times (Green Forest, AR: New Leaf Press, 2000). Second edition in 2015.

Wrath and Glory: Unveiling the Majestic Book of Revelation (Green Forest, AR: New Leaf Press, 2001). Second edition in 2016.

America the Beautiful? The United States in Bible Prophecy (McKinney, TX: Lamb & Lion Ministries, 2003). Second edition in 2006. Third edition in 2009.

God's Plan for the Ages: The Blueprint of Bible Prophecy (McKinney, TX: Lamb & Lion Ministries, 2005).

Eternity: Heaven or Hell? (McKinney, TX: Lamb & Lion Ministries, 2010).

Jesus: The Lamb and The Lion (McKinney, TX: Lamb & Lion Ministries, 2011).

The Man of Lawlessness: The Antichrist in the Tribulation (McKinney, TX: Lamb & Lion Ministries, 2012).

A Prophetic Manifesto (McKinney, TX: Lamb & Lion Ministries, 2012).

Living on Borrowed Time: the Imminent Return of Jesus (McKinney, TX: Lamb & Lion Ministries, 2013).

The Jewish People: Rejected or Beloved? (McKinney, TX: Lamb & Lion Ministries, 2014).

Preface

God's love for the Jewish people is clearly demonstrated in the chronicle of His faithfulness in fulfilling the promises contained in the prophecies He has given them through their prophets. It is a story of amazing grace, and that is why it is so important to the Church.

Tragically, for the past 2,000 years, the Church at large — even today — has taken the position that because of the unfaithfulness of the Jewish people to God's call on their lives to be a witness of Him, He has disinherited them, cancelled His promises to them and nullified His prophecies concerning them. This is called Replacement Theology, and as I have shown in my book, *The Jewish People: Rejected or Beloved?* this abhorrent theology is just not biblical.

The advocates of Replacement Theology respond by proclaiming, "In Old Testament times, the Jewish people rejected God as King of their nation, and in New Testament times, they rejected God's Son as their Messiah. Therefore, they do not deserve for God to be faithful to His promises and prophecies concerning them."

My response to this argument is that none of us have been faithful to God. All of us are sinners who deserve nothing but death. God's relationship with Israel is a demonstration of His grace — a manifestation of unmerited love. And in that regard, the Jewish people to this day remain a witness of what it means to have a relationship with God. Thus, from their history, we can see that when we are faithful, He blesses. When we are unfaithful, He disciplines. And when we repent, He forgives and forgets and begins to bless again.

My previous book on the Jewish people showed how God has been faithful to all the promises He has made to them, despite their unfaithfulness, for the Bible says that God is faithful even when we are unfaithful (2 Timothy 2:13).

This book will clearly show that God has also been faithful in fulfilling the prophecies He has given to the Jewish prophets concerning the future of their people to this day. And because of that, we can be assured that God will fulfill all the prophecies concerning Israel that are yet future — and the prophecies yet to be fulfilled are mind-boggling!

I pray that as you read this book, your heart will be touched anew by the unfathomable grace of God. Any god created by the mind of Man would have given up on the stubborn and rebellious Jewish people a long time ago, but not the true God of this universe.

I also hope you will be encouraged to believe that just as God has been faithful in fulfilling every prophecy given to the Jewish people, He will also be faithful in fulfilling every prophecy He has given to the Church.

I pray too that if any reader has any vestige of Replacement Theology in his or her heart or any tinge of anti-Semitism, this book will deliver them from it.

Let us all keep in mind that he who mistreats the Jewish people "touches the apple of God's eye" (Zechariah 2:8).

Dr. David R. Reagan
Allen, Texas
January 2017

Prologue

Since many who read this book may not be familiar with biblical history, I thought it would be important to begin with a brief overview of the ancient origins of the Jewish people.

Their birth as a nation began with an event that took place almost 4,000 years ago in a place in the Middle East called Ur of the Chaldees (in the southern part of modern day Iraq).

The Call of Abram

God called a man named Abram to step out in faith and move his family to a new land that would be revealed to him in due time (Genesis 12:1-3):

> 1) Now the LORD said to Abram, "Go forth from your country, and from your relatives and from your father's house, to the land which I will show you;
>
> 2) and I will make you a great nation, and I will bless you, and make your name great; and so you shall be a blessing;
>
> 3) and I will bless those who bless you, and the one who curses you I will curse. And in you all the families of the earth will be blessed."

Abram responded in faith to the Lord's call on his life by embarking on a long journey that ultimately led him to the land of Canaan (where modern day Israel is located). After his arrival in the land, God changed his name from Abram, meaning, "exalted father," to Abraham, meaning "father of a multitude" (Genesis 17:5).

Abraham's Descendants

God's promises to Abraham were repeated to him in whole or in part a total of six times (Genesis 12:7; 13:14-16; 15:1-6; 15:17-21; 17:1-8 and 22:17-18). They were reconfirmed to Abraham's son, Isaac, in Genesis 26:1-5, and to Isaac's son, Jacob, in Genesis 28:10-15.

Later, God changed Jacob's name to Israel, meaning "he who wrestles with God" (Genesis 35:9-12). This name was to prove prophetic in nature, for both Jacob and his descendants were to have a tumultuous relationship with God. A total of 12 sons were born to Jacob and his wives, and collectively they and their descendants came to be called "the children of Israel" (Deuteronomy 1:3).

The Descent into Egypt

One of Jacob's sons, Joseph, was his favorite, and the other sons, acting out of jealousy, decided to sell him into slavery. A caravan headed to Egypt purchased him. The brothers then led their father to believe that Joseph had been killed by a wild animal.

Years later, through a bizarre series of circumstances, in what is one of the most remarkable stories in the Bible (Genesis 37-41), Joseph became the vizier of Egypt, a position equivalent to being the Pharaoh's prime minister (Genesis 41:45).

Seven years after Joseph acquired his position of authority, the land of Egypt and all the biblical lands of the Middle East were afflicted with a terrible famine. Joseph had prophesied this famine and had prepared Egypt for it by storing up food for seven years. When Jacob heard there was food available in Egypt, he sent his sons to purchase some of it (Genesis 42:1-13). Joseph recognized his brothers, forgave them of their treachery, and invited the entire family to move to Egypt (Genesis 45:16-19).

God prepared Jacob (now known as Israel) for Joseph's invitation by speaking to him in a vision (Genesis 46:3-4):

> 3) He [God] said, "I am God, the God of your father; do not be afraid to go down to Egypt, for I will make you a great nation there.
>
> 4) "I will go down with you to Egypt, and I will also surely bring you up again; and Joseph will close your eyes."

And so, in about 1875 BC, the 75 members of Jacob's extended family (Acts 7:14) migrated to Egypt where they took up residence in the land of Goshen (Genesis 45:10). This was an area of Egypt located in the eastern delta of the Nile River.

Egyptian Bondage

The Bible says they "were fruitful and increased greatly, and multiplied, and became exceedingly mighty, so that the land was filled with them" (Exodus 1:7). But the very next verse records an ominous development: "Now a new king arose over Egypt who did not know Joseph" (Exodus 1:8).

Fearing the rapid growth of these foreigners in his land, the new Pharaoh decided to enslave them and submit them to forced labor (Exodus 1:9-14). For the next 400 years the children of Israel endured this terrible bondage until God raised up a deliverer from their midst — a man by the name of Moses.

God empowered Moses to confront Pharaoh and demand the release of the Israelites. Through a series of calamities inflicted upon the land of Egypt by God through Moses, Pharaoh finally relented and allowed the children of Israel to depart the land (Exodus 7-11). By that time, their numbers had increased to over 600,000 men, indicating a total population, including women and children, of more than 2.5 million (Exodus 12:37-38).

In approximately 1446 BC, Moses led the Jewish people out of Egypt, beginning a journey to the land God had promised them in Canaan.[1] The journey should have taken 11 days (Deuteronomy 1:2). But, instead, it took them 40 years!

The extended length of the journey was due to the people's lack of faith that ultimately motivated some of them to rebel against Moses (Numbers 14:1-4 and Psalm 78:17-42). This behavior prompted God to decide that the generation that departed from Egypt would have to die in the wilderness before their descendants would be allowed to enter the Promised Land (Numbers 14:26-38).

The Mosaic Covenant

While the children of Israel were wandering in the desert, God appeared to Moses on Mount Sinai and gave him the nation's moral law in the form of the Ten Commandments (Exodus 20:1-17). God also gave Moses many other civil and ceremonial laws, including very specific instructions about how to build a portable temple that would serve as their worship center — The Tabernacle of Moses (Exodus 21-30; Leviticus 1-27; Numbers 2-9,15,18-19,28-30,35-36 and Deuteronomy 5,14-27).

Another very significant development during the wilderness wanderings was a declaration by God that He had selected the children of Israel to be His Chosen People to serve as a witness of Him to all the Gentile nations. This was, of course, simply another way in which the Lord reaffirmed the covenant He had made with Abraham. This declaration is found in Deuteronomy 7:6-9:

> 6) For you are a holy people to the LORD your God; the LORD your God has chosen you to be a people for His own possession out

> of all the peoples who are on the face of the earth.
>
> 7) The LORD did not set His love on you nor choose you because you were more in number than any of the peoples, for you were the fewest of all peoples,
>
> 8) but because the LORD loved you and kept the oath which He swore to your forefathers, the LORD brought you out by a mighty hand and redeemed you from the house of slavery, from the hand of Pharaoh king of Egypt.
>
> 9) Know therefore that the LORD your God, He is God, the faithful God, who keeps His covenant and His lovingkindness to a thousandth generation with those who love Him and keep His commandments . . .

The Land Use Covenant

It was about 1406 BC when the children of Israel were finally poised to cross the Jordan River and enter the land they had been promised. On that auspicious occasion, Moses paused their journey to summarize God's Law for them (Deuteronomy 5-27). He also used the occasion to provide them with some detailed warnings (Deuteronomy 28-29).

As he presented these warnings, Moses emphasized that although God had given the children of Israel an everlasting deed to the land, their enjoyment of it would depend on their obedience to the Mosaic Covenant.

One of Moses' strongest warnings concerned the danger of intermarrying with the Canaanites because it would lead the Jewish people into idolatry (Deuteronomy 7:1-5).

Moses proclaimed that if the people were obedient to God, He would shower them with blessings (Deuteronomy

28:1-14). Their children, their crops and their animals would be blessed (28:4). Their enemies would be defeated and they would "abound in prosperity" and be established as "a holy people" whom the rest of the world would fear (28:7-11).

Moses proceeded to sternly warn them that if they were disobedient to God, He would place curses on them. Their children would rebel, their crops would fail and their animals would not reproduce (Deuteronomy 28:16-19). They would also suffer from diseases, drought, and foreign domination (28:21,24,33).

Moses further warned that if they did not respond in repentance to these remedial judgments, the Lord would intensify them: ". . . then the LORD will bring extraordinary plagues on you and your descendants, even severe and lasting plagues, and miserable and chronic sicknesses . . . all the diseases of Egypt of which you were afraid . . ." (28:59-60).

Moses then declared that if these extreme measures did not produce repentance, God would subject them to the worst possible punishment — exile from their homeland: "Moreover, the LORD will scatter you among all peoples, from one end of the earth to the other end of the earth; and there you shall serve other gods, wood and stone, which you or your fathers have not known" (Deuteronomy 28:64).

Moses had already briefly mentioned this ultimate punishment of God in the survey of the Law which He had presented in the book of Leviticus. After listing many possible remedial judgments (Leviticus 26:14-32), just as in Deuteronomy, Moses warned that God's ultimate judgment would be their "scattering among the nations" (26:33).

Arrival in the Promised Land

The children of Israel entered their Promised Land under the leadership of Moses' successor, Joshua, who had served as the commander-in-chief of Moses' armies (Exodus 17:8-

13). They launched their conquest of the land with specific instructions from God that they were to annihilate the Canaanite peoples (Deuteronomy 20:16-17). This command was given to prevent them from becoming contaminated by the evil, pagan ways of the Canaanites (Exodus 34:12-16).

The conquest of the land extended over the next 130 years, during which time the Israelites stopped short of exterminating the Canaanites. The result was exactly what Moses had warned — the children of Israel started intermarrying with the Canaanites, and they became heavily involved in idolatry (Judges 2:11-14):

> 11) Then the sons of Israel did evil in the sight of the LORD and served the Baals,
>
> 12) and they forsook the LORD, the God of their fathers, who had brought them out of the land of Egypt, and followed other gods from among the gods of the peoples who were around them, and bowed themselves down to them; thus they provoked the LORD to anger.
>
> 13) So they forsook the LORD and served Baal and the Ashtaroth.
>
> 14) The anger of the LORD burned against Israel, and He gave them into the hands of plunderers who plundered them; and He sold them into the hands of their enemies around them, so that they could no longer stand before their enemies.

The Jewish people were disciplined by the Lord, but He did not abandon them. Instead, He raised up leaders called judges who served as deliverers, calling the people to repentance and organizing them to defeat their persecutors.

The Period of the Judges

During the next 400 years, God reigned over Israel through a series of 16 judges. The book of Judges in the Bible reveals a very definite pattern of behavior on the part of the Israelites that repeated itself over and over again. They would lapse into apostasy through the worship of idols. The Lord would respond by sending an enemy like the Philistines to attack them and even conquer them. When the people would turn back to the Lord in repentance, He would raise up a judge to deliver them (Psalm 106:40-45).

The greatest of the judges of Israel was Samuel. Near the end of his judgeship, the people came to him and demanded that he find and anoint a person to serve as king of the nation (1 Samuel 8:4-9). Samuel responded by warning the people that a human king would abuse them and their children in many different ways and that he would burden them with oppressive taxes (1 Samuel 8:10-18). But the people would not listen. They demanded a king so "that we also may be like all the nations" (1 Samuel 8:19-20).

For Israel to one day have a king had always been a part of God's plan for the nation. Jacob had prophesied that a time would come when they would be ruled by a king from the tribe of Judah (Genesis 49:8-12). And the Law of Moses outlined the royal responsibilities of a king (Deuteronomy 17:14-20). The problem was that the children of Israel demanded a king long before the proper time and for the wrong motivation. God desired that they be a very special nation that would witness His glory to all the world. They wanted, instead, to be like all the other nations.

The Reign of Kings

Samuel reluctantly supplied the people with exactly the kind of king they wanted. He picked a handsome man named Saul who was head and shoulders taller than any other man in the land (1 Samuel 9:2). He was from the wrong tribe — the tribe of Benjamin (1 Samuel 9:1-2). And he proved to have many character faults. He had a jealous spirit about him, he was subject to fits of depression and he often acted rashly, without consulting the Lord.

Saul got caught up in a downward spiral that ended with him consulting mediums and trafficking in spirits of the dead — all in violation of God's laws. Tragically, he ended his life by committing suicide on the battlefield by falling on his own sword (1 Samuel 31:1-4).

The United Kingdom

Saul's place was taken by David, a man God had already raised up to succeed him. He had been selected by God, not on the basis of his external appearance, but on the condition of his heart (1 Samuel 16:7). He had been anointed by Samuel (1 Samuel 16:13), so he was a king-in-waiting at the time of Saul's death. He was also from the correct tribe — the kingly tribe of Judah. David, who proved to be a great warrior, became king in about 1010 BC and proceeded to bring the 12 tribes of Israel together into a united kingdom.

One of David's most important accomplishments was his conquest of the city of Jerusalem which had remained under the control of the Jebusites (2 Samuel 5:6-7). Equally important, he purchased Mount Moriah (2 Samuel 24:18-24) which was located on the north side of the city. He turned this mount into the worship center of the nation by bringing the Ark of the Covenant to Jerusalem (2 Samuel 6:12-19) and placing it in a simple tent located on the mount. Worship was conducted at this site 24 hours a day (1 Chronicles 16:37). David succeeded in uniting all the Jewish tribes around the city of Jerusalem, which became the political and spiritual capital of the nation.

David earnestly desired to build a permanent Temple of the Lord to replace the Tabernacle tent that served in that capacity, but God refused to allow him to proceed with his plans because he had spilled too much blood through his various military conquests (1 Chronicles 28:3). David was told that his son, Solomon, would be given the blessing of building the Temple.

David died after reigning for 40 years. He was succeeded by his son, Solomon, in about 970 BC. Solomon was granted great wisdom by God (2 Chronicles 1:7-12), and he used that wisdom to proceed to build and dedicate the Temple. Under his reign, he brought the nation to its highest glory (2 Chronicles 9:20).

The Divided Kingdom

But when Solomon died 40 years into his reign, his son, Rehoboam began to act rashly, and the people of Israel rebelled (2 Chronicles 10). They turned to a rebel leader named Jeroboam who united the ten northern tribes into a state called Israel whose capital was ultimately established in the central hill country at a place called Samaria.[2]

Rehoboam was left with two tribes in the south, Judah and Benjamin. His nation took the name of Judah, with its capital in Jerusalem.

And so, the kingdom of David and Solomon split and remained in that condition for the next 208 years, until the northern kingdom of Israel was conquered by the Assyrians in 722 BC.

This brings us to where the story resumes in chapter 1 with the worldwide dispersion of the Jewish people that began with the conquest of the northern kingdom of Israel.

The Sections of This Book

In the pages to follow, we will take a look at four prophecies about the Jewish people that were fulfilled between 722 BC and the beginning of the 20th Century. Next, we will consider seven prophecies that were fulfilled in whole or in part during the 20th Century. We will conclude by taking a

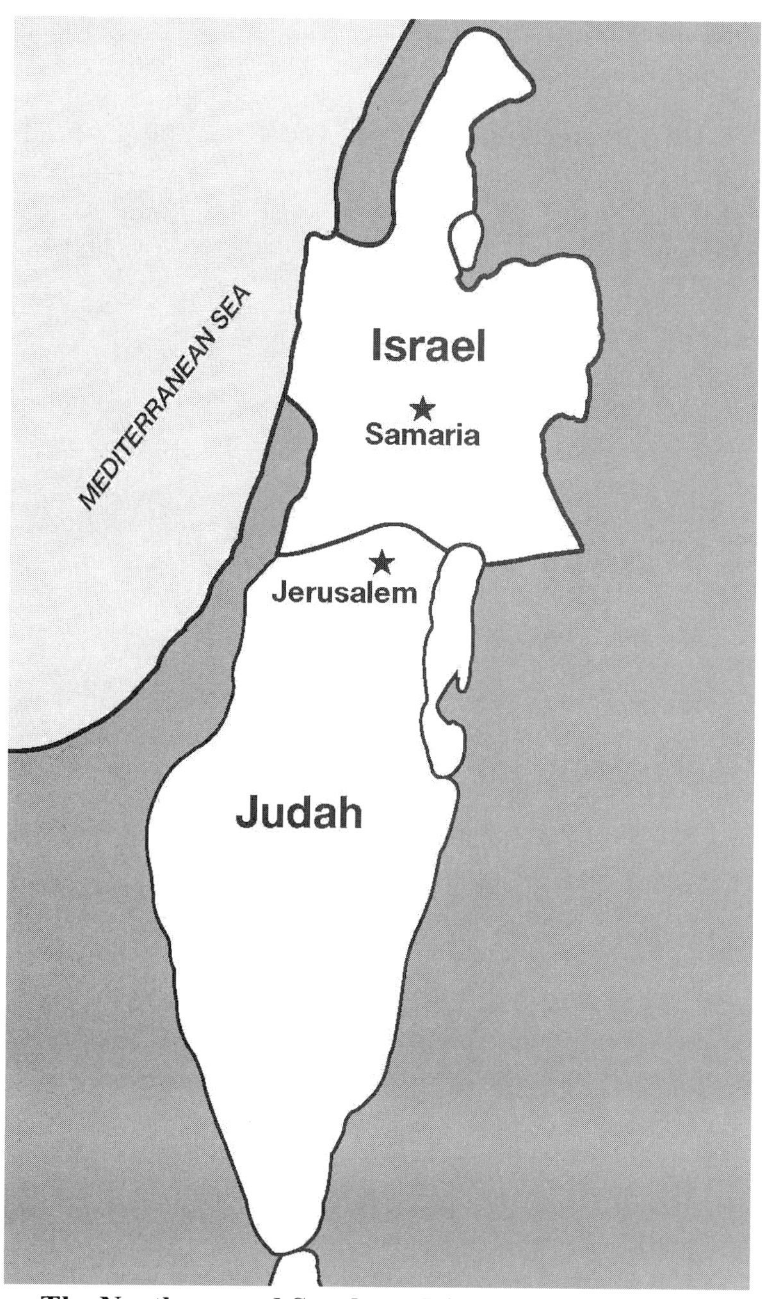

The Northern and Southern Kingdoms of the Jews after Solomon.

look at the many prophecies concerning Israel that are yet to be fulfilled in these end times.

This prophetic panorama of Israel in Bible prophecy should prove to be inspiring and spiritually enriching to you, for it clearly reveals the sovereignty of God in history, His faithfulness to all His promises, His patience and lovingkindness, and His amazing grace.

Part 1

The Past

Chapter 1

The Worldwide Dispersion of the Jews

While the children of Israel were wandering in the wilderness, before their entrance into the Promised Land, God made it clear to them through Moses that although the land had been given to them as an eternal possession, their use and enjoyment of it would depend on their faithfulness to Him.

Moses also warned them that if they strayed from God's Law, prophets would be sent to call them to repentance, and if they ignored the prophets, God would send remedial judgments (see pages 13-14).

Tragically, once they entered the Promised Land, it did not take long before the Israelites got their eyes off the Lord. They began to intermarry with the Canaanites, and they were led astray into idolatry.

And just as He had warned through Moses, God responded to Israel's persistent rebellion by sending remedial judgments and raising up prophetic voices to call the people to repentance.

The Prophets to Israel

Seventy years into the history of the northern kingdom of Israel, the prophet Elijah suddenly appeared on the scene. He confronted the evil king Ahab and his wife, Jezebel, and he called the whole nation to repentance, saying (1 Kings 18:21):

> How long will you hesitate between two opinions? If the LORD is God, follow him; but if Baal, follow him.

Even though both the leaders and the people of Israel refused to respond in repentance, God in His patience continued to warn. Next, He called an unusual man to speak His warning — a fig-picker from the rural village of Tekoa in Judah. It would be like God calling a cowboy from Calgary, Canada today to deliver a prophetic message to the President of the United States!

His name was Amos, and although he was an uneducated man, he was a fearless and obedient servant of God. He proceeded to read the riot act to the people of Israel (Amos 2:6-8 — *The Living Bible Paraphrased*):

> 6) The Lord says, "The people of Israel have sinned again and again, and I will not forget it. I will not leave them unpunished any more. For they have perverted justice by accepting bribes and sold into slavery the poor who can't repay their debts; they trade them for a pair of shoes.
>
> 7) "They trample the poor in the dust and kick aside the meek. And a man and his father defile the same temple-girl, corrupting My holy name.
>
> 8) "At their religious feasts they lounge in clothing stolen from their debtors, and in My own Temple they offer sacrifices of wine they purchased with stolen money."

Amos even had the audacity to attack the sinful, greedy women of Israel, calling them "fat cows of Bashan" (Amos 4:1 — LBP).

The prophet was particularly appalled by the religious hypocrisy that was rampant in the land. He pointed out that despite all their religiosity, they lived like pagans and denied social justice to the poor (Amos 5:21-24).

He reminded them of the many remedial judgments God had sent — including drought, famine, mildew, locusts, pestilence and defeat in wars (Amos 4:6-11). He concluded by declaring that if the nation persisted in its rebellion, God "will destroy it from the face of the earth" (Amos 9:8).

Israel's Final Prophet

But they did not listen. So, God raised up another prophet from among their own people — a man by the name of Hosea. For the next 20 years, right up to the time of the kingdom's destruction, Hosea called the people to repentance. And like Amos, he confronted them with a litany of their sins, beginning with these words (Hosea 4:1-3):

> 1) Listen to the word of the LORD, O sons of Israel, for the LORD has a case against the inhabitants of the land, because there is no faithfulness or kindness or knowledge of God in the land.
>
> 2) There is swearing, deception, murder, stealing and adultery. They employ violence, so that bloodshed follows bloodshed.
>
> 3) Therefore the land mourns, and everyone who lives in it languishes along with the beasts of the field and the birds of the sky, and also the fish of the sea disappear.

Hosea focused on the sin of idolatry, referring to it vividly as "the spirit of harlotry" (Hosea 4:12 and 9:1). And like Amos, he also railed against the people's religious hypocrisy, proclaiming: "For I delight in loyalty rather than sacrifice, and in the knowledge of God rather than burnt offerings"

(6:6).

Hosea pleaded with his fellow countrymen to "return, O Israel, to the LORD your God" (14:1), and he warned specifically that if they failed to do so, God would destroy their kingdom through the Assyrians (11:5-6). He also pointed out that should this happen, they would have no one to blame except themselves (13:9).

Meanwhile, in Judah, the prophet Isaiah, who was called by God to be a prophet to his own kingdom, also issued a warning to Israel. He cried out, "Woe to the proud crown [the capital city of Samaria] of the drunkards of Ephraim [the kingdom of Israel]" (Isaiah 28:1). He then declared that God was raising up "a mighty agent" to destroy the kingdom (28:2). This was, of course, a reference to the Assyrians whom Isaiah had referred to earlier as "the rod of God's anger" (10:5).

I think it is fascinating to note that near the end of the reign of Israel's very first king, Jeroboam, a prophet named Abijah had prophesied the ultimate destruction of the kingdom of Israel: "For the LORD will strike Israel, as a reed is shaken in the water; and He will uproot Israel from this good land which He gave to their fathers, and will scatter them beyond the Euphrates River, because they have made their Asherim, provoking the LORD to anger" (1 Kings 14:15 — Asherim were totem poles that were erected to honor the female God named Asherah).

The Destruction of Israel

All these appeals and warnings fell on deaf ears. The result was the destruction of the kingdom of Israel by the Assyrians in 722 BC. The kingdom had lasted 208 years. There had been 19 kings, and not a single one had been considered righteous in the eyes of God.

The reasons for their destruction are summed up in 2 Kings 17: "They set for themselves sacred pillars and Asherim on every high hill and under every green tree" (10), "they burned incense on all the high places" (11), "they served idols" (12), "they made for themselves molten images . . . and worshiped all the host of heaven and served Baal" (16), and "they made their sons and their daughters pass through the fire, and practiced divination and enchantments" (17).

The Assyrian conquest of the kingdom of Israel marked the beginning of the dispersion of the Jewish people in accordance with the prophecy of Deuteronomy 28:63-64. The ten Jewish tribes of that kingdom ultimately ended up being scattered all across the Eurasian continent, from Assyria to China and even into the Indian subcontinent.[1]

The Kingdom of Judah

The southern kingdom of Judah began with King Rehoboam who was the rightful heir to the throne, since he was the son of Solomon, but he veered off the path of righteousness, and his son, Abijah (also known as Abijam), followed in his steps.

It was not until the 20th year of the kingdom that a good king by the name of Asa ascended the throne. He reigned for 41 years and was followed by his righteous son, Jehoshaphat, who ruled for 25 years.

It was up and down after that with regard to the kings, but overall, there was a steady descent of the society into spiritual darkness. It is a tragic story because no other nation had ever been blessed as much as Judah. God prospered its people and gave them many righteous kings. More important, His Shekinah Glory resided in their Temple in Jerusalem. But the people of Judah took their eyes off the Lord and began to wallow in pride, which led them into a multiplicity of sins.

The Prophets to Judah

The earliest prophet to speak out against Judah's increasing apostasy was Joel. He appeared on the scene during the reign of King Uzziah (783-732 BC) when the kingdom was almost 150 years old. This would have been before the fall of the northern kingdom of Israel.

Judah had just experienced a terrible locust invasion that had made waste of the kingdom's agricultural production. The nation was facing famine. Joel's message was a tough one. Basically, he said, "If you think this locust invasion is bad, just wait and see what God has in store for you if you do not repent." He then warned that God was going to send an army that would do far greater damage than the locusts.

He cried out to his people in behalf of God, saying, "Return to Me with all your heart, and with fasting, weeping and mourning; and rend your heart and not your garments" (Joel 2:12-13).

Isaiah's Message

In the year of King Uzziah's death (740 BC), God called Isaiah to be a prophet to Judah (Isaiah 6:1). As his first assignment, the Lord instructed him to make an inventory of the kingdom's sins.

The list appears in Isaiah 5, and it is an alarming one. It included injustice, greed, pleasure seeking, blasphemy, moral perversion, intellectual pride, intemperance and political corruption (Isaiah 5:7-23). And keep in mind that this list was compiled at the end of the 52 year reign of a righteous king!

The cause of all this spiritual pollution was summed up by Isaiah in the following words: "For they have rejected the law of the LORD of hosts, and despised the word of the Holy One of Israel" (Isaiah 5:24).

Isaiah pulled no punches in warning Judah of the consequences of its sins, if the nation refused to repent. He pointed to what had happened to Israel: “Shall I not do to Jerusalem and her images just as I have done to Samaria and her idols?” (Isaiah 10:11). He even prophesied that Babylon would be the empire that would destroy Judah, referring to the Babylonians as His “consecrated ones” and His “mighty warriors” (Isaiah 13:3).

The Message of Jeremiah

In 626 BC, about 60 years after Isaiah’s death, God called the prophet Jeremiah to take his place. And once again, the Lord instructed him, like Isaiah, to begin his ministry by compiling an inventory of the kingdom’s sins (Jeremiah 5:1-2).

When Jeremiah reported back, the list he had compiled was identical to Isaiah’s (Jeremiah 5-10), except that he added the sin of religious corruption: “An appalling and horrible thing has happened in the land: The prophets prophesy falsely, and the priests rule on their own authority . . .” (5:30-31).

Jeremiah’s report contained three graphic summary statements:

1) “They have made their faces harder than rock” (5:3).
2) They have “stubborn and rebellious hearts” (5:23).
3) They do not “even know how to blush” (6:15).

Jeremiah then went forth to call for repentance and to warn of impending destruction. He began his ministry by preaching a powerful sermon in the Temple in Jerusalem. He called upon the people to amend their ways and practice judgment, or else their Temple would be destroyed (7:1-7). He then asked them a piercing question (7:9-10):

> 9) “Will you steal, murder, and commit adultery and swear falsely, and offer sacrifices to Baal and walk after other gods that you have not known,

> 10) then come and stand before Me in this house, which is called by My name, and say, 'We are delivered!' — that you may do all these abominations?"

The religious leaders reacted in outrage, banning Jeremiah from the Temple (36:5). The people mocked him, claiming that God would never allow anyone to destroy the Temple that was inhabited by His Shekinah Glory (7:4).

Jeremiah never let up in his call for repentance and his pronouncement of warnings. And the people of Judah never wavered in their hostile response. He was attacked by his brothers (12:6), imprisoned (37:18), beaten and put in stocks (20:1-2), thrown into a cistern (38:6), denounced by a false prophet (28:1ff) and constantly threatened with death (38:4).

Jeremiah was very specific with his warnings (20:4-5):

> 4) For thus says the LORD, ". . . I will give over all Judah to the hand of the king of Babylon, and he will carry them away as exiles to Babylon and will slay them with the sword.
>
> 5) "I will also give over all the wealth of this city, all its produce and all its costly things; even all the treasures of the kings of Judah I will give over to the hand of their enemies, and they will plunder them, take them away and bring them to Babylon."

Not only did he specify that the nation would be destroyed by Babylon and that the people would be carried away to captivity, he also stated that this exile would last exactly 70 years (25:11-12). But all the warnings fell on deaf ears. Here's how the response is described in Jeremiah 17:23 — "Yet they did not listen or incline their ears, but stiffened their necks in order not to listen or take correction."

The Destruction by Babylon

So, God sent the Babylonians as His "war club" (51:20), and they destroyed Jerusalem and the Temple. Most of the residents of Jerusalem were either killed or captured and sent into exile. Many others, who were able to escape or who were left behind, decided to flee to Egypt (43:1-7).

The conquest of the city of Jerusalem and the destruction of the kingdom of Judah produced two of the saddest verses in the Hebrew Scriptures (2 Chronicles 36:15-16):

> 15) The LORD, the God of their fathers, sent word to them again and again by His messengers, because He had compassion on His people and on His dwelling place;
>
> 16) but they continually mocked the messengers of God, despised His words and scoffed at His prophets, until the wrath of the LORD arose against His people, until there was no remedy.

The Babylonian captivity (608 - 538 BC) produced the second great Jewish dispersion — to Babylon and Egypt. And when the Jews were allowed to return to their homeland 70 years later by the Persian King Cyrus, the majority decided to remain in Babylon.[2]

The Widespread Dispersion of the Jews

Shortly before the time of Jesus, in the late First Century BC, a Greek geographer named Strabo stated that you could not go anywhere in the civilized world without encountering a Jew.[3] By the time of Jesus in the First Century AD, scholars estimate that the majority of the Jewish people (more than 5 million) were living in the Diaspora.[4] The Egyptian city of Alexandria was 40 per cent Jewish, amounting to approximately one million Jews.[5]

The widespread dispersion of the Jews at the beginning of the First Century AD is attested to in the New Testament. On the Day of Pentecost in about 30 AD, when the Apostle Peter preached the first Gospel sermon, a great multitude of Jews from the Diaspora had gathered in Jerusalem for the feast days (Acts 2:9-11):

> 9) Parthians and Medes and Elamites, and residents of Mesopotamia, Judea and Cappadocia, Pontus and Asia,
>
> 10) Phrygia and Pamphylia, Egypt and the districts of Libya around Cyrene, and visitors from Rome, both Jews and proselytes,
>
> 11) Cretans and Arabs . . .

Also in the New Testament you can find a reference to "the Diaspora among the Greeks" in John 7:35. The book of James is addressed "to the twelve tribes who are dispersed abroad . . ." (James 1:1). Likewise, Peter's first epistle is addressed to "those who reside as aliens, scattered throughout Pontus, Galatia, Cappadocia, Asia and Bithynia . . ." (1 Peter 1:1).

And then, there is the story of the Ethiopian Eunuch in Acts 8. He was a Black Jew from Africa who had come to Jerusalem to worship. As he was traveling back home, he encountered a Christian evangelist by the name of Philip who shared the Gospel with him. The man accepted Jesus as his Savior, was baptized and went on his way rejoicing — becoming one of the first African converts to Christianity (Acts 8:26-40).

The Destruction by the Romans

In 63 BC, Judah became a protectorate of Rome, and in 6 AD, the kingdom was reorganized as a Roman province.[6]

Roman rule proved to be harsh. The Jews were heavily taxed, and their religion and culture were held in contempt. The Jewish people were particularly outraged when the Romans took over the appointment of the High Priest, resulting in the selection of Roman collaborators.[7]

"Ultimately, the combination of financial exploitation, Rome's unbridled contempt for Judaism, and the unabashed favoritism that the Romans extended to Gentiles" brought about a Jewish revolt in 66 AD.[8]

The revolt led to a siege of Jerusalem by Roman troops. After a stand-off of almost five months, the Romans finally breached the walls in 70 AD and then systematically destroyed the city and its temple. In the process, they slaughtered tens of thousands of its inhabitants.

But this great tragedy failed to quell the rebellious spirit of the Jews. Fifty-two years later, they rose up in rebellion once again in a well-organized guerilla campaign that lasted three years (132 - 135 AD).

This revolt proved to be the last straw for the Romans. Hadrian, the Roman Emperor, responded brutally. According to Roman historian Cassius Dio (c. 150 - 235 AD), 580,000 Jews were killed, and 50 fortified towns and 985 villages were razed to the ground.[9] Those who were not killed were sold into slavery.

Additionally, Hadrian ordered Jews to be banned from Jerusalem, except on the day of Tisha B'Av (the day of mourning over the destruction of the first two temples). He changed the name of Jerusalem to *Aelia Capitolina* (after his family name, Aelius, and the Capitoline Triad of gods — Jupiter, Juno and Minerva).[10] And he changed the name of the Jewish homeland from Judah to Syria Palestina (Palestina being the Latin name for the Jew's ancient enemies, the Philistines).[11]

Worldwide Dispersion

The ultimate result of the destruction of the kingdom of Judah was the worldwide dispersion of the remaining Jewish people. Yes, there were small pockets of Jews who remained in their homeland, settling mainly in the Galilee and in the city of Tiberias. But the vast majority were scattered to foreign nations — all of which was in fulfillment of very specific warnings God had supplied through His prophets over a thousand years before.

The Jewish historian, Josephus, writing near the end of the First Century AD, stated: "There is no city, no tribe, whether Greek or barbarian, in which Jewish law and Jewish customs have not taken root."[12]

By the end of the Middle Ages (400 to 1400 AD), there were four identifiable groups of Jews in the Diaspora:

1) The Ashkenazi Jews of Central and Eastern Europe.[13]

2) The Sephardic Jews of the Iberian Peninsula (Portugal and Spain).[14]

3) The Mizrahi Jews of Persia.[15]

4) The Anusim Jews which consisted of those who were compelled to convert to either Christianity or Islam.[16] They were sometimes referred to as "Crypto-Jews."

Each of these groups, in their isolation from each other over the years, developed distinctive forms of dress, worship and language.[17] With regard to language, Hebrew became the language of the synagogue. It ceased to be spoken in daily conversation. Among the Ashkenazim, they combined German with Hebrew to produce a language called Yiddish.[18] The Sephardim, on the other hand, combined Spanish with Hebrew to produce Ladino.[19]

In 1492, when the Jews were expelled from Spain, the Sephardic communities migrated to North Africa and throughout the Ottoman Empire. Later, some of them even went to the newly discovered Latin America.

This subsequent dispersion into the Ottoman Empire resulted in the growth of Mizrahi Jews, because that term came to be applied to those who ended up living in areas dominated by Muslims. As would be expected, they developed a mixed language called Judeo-Arabic.[20]

For 600 years, Babylon was the center of the Diaspora, from the 5th to the 11th Centuries. During the 11th Century, Jewish migration shifted the center of the Diaspora population to Spain, France and the Rhineland, where it remained until the 15th Century. At that point, expulsions and offers of refuge led the Jews either to Poland or the Ottoman Empire. Those two regions remained the principal centers of Jewish life until the 19th Century.

During the 19th Century, the Jews in the Diaspora began to migrate in significant numbers to the Western Hemisphere, including South America. Between 1840 and 1939, the Jewish population of North and South America increased from 1.1% of the world's Jews to 33.1%.[21] During that same time period, worldwide Jewry increased from 4.5 million to 16.7 million.[22]

Jewish Demographics

The Nazi Holocaust resulted in the deaths of 6 million Jews, including 1.5 million children. This reduced the worldwide population of Jews to approximately 10 million. Since that time, the population has grown to 14 million, with 6.5 million now residing in the re-established state of Israel.[23]

According to Roman records, there were about 8 to 10 million Jews in the First Century. Since that time, the population of China has grown from 30 million to over one billion. Based on growth statistics like this, demographers estimate that there should be 400 to 500 million Jews alive in the world today.[24]

Instead, there are only about 4 million more today than 2,000 years ago. This fact is the fulfillment of a prophecy found in Deuteronomy 4:27 — "And the LORD will scatter you among the peoples, and you shall be left few in number among the nations, where the LORD drives you." That prophecy was delivered by Moses over 3,400 years ago!

Prophecies Fulfilled

The Jewish people have been dispersed all over the world, just as God warned they would be if they were not faithful to Him. Likewise, as I will show in chapter 2, they have been severely persecuted everywhere they have gone — again, in fulfillment of a prophecy delivered by Moses (Deuteronomy 28:65-67):

> 65) Among those nations [where the Jews will be scattered] you shall find no rest, and there will be no resting place for the sole of your foot; but there the LORD will give you a trembling heart, failing of eyes, and despair of soul.
>
> 66) So your life shall hang in doubt before you; and you will be in dread night and day, and shall have no assurance of your life.
>
> 67) In the morning you shall say, "Would that it were evening!" And at evening you shall say, "Would that it were morning!" because of the dread of your heart which you dread, and for the sight of your eyes which you will see.

The great miracle of the Diaspora is that the Jewish people have survived to this day — again, in fulfillment of Bible prophecy (Jeremiah 30:11):

> "For I am with you," declares the LORD, "to save you; for I will destroy completely all the nations where I have scattered you, only I will not destroy you completely. But I will chasten you justly and will by no means leave you unpunished."

We will take a look at this miracle of preservation in chapter 3.

A Warning to America

Let me conclude by emphasizing a point that I have made many times, particularly in my book, *America the Beautiful?*[25] It is the fact that I am convinced that ancient Judah is a prophetic type of the United States.

Just like Judah, God has blessed us with great leaders, freedom and prosperity. More important, just like Judah, our nation was founded upon God's Word. And just as God blessed Judah with His spiritual presence in the nation's temple, He has given America the great spiritual blessing of spreading the Gospel all over the world.

Yet, despite our blessings, we have responded just like Judah with pride, apostasy and rebellion. And just as with Judah, God has been calling us to repentance and warning us of impending destruction through remedial judgments like 9/11 and through prophetic voices like Dave Wilkerson.

And just as the people of Judah laughed at the warnings and said, "God dwells in our temple and would never allow an enemy to destroy our nation," the people of America are saying, "God sits on His throne wrapped in an American flag and will never allow us to be destroyed."

We need to remember the words of the prophet Nahum:

> The LORD is slow to anger and great in power, And the LORD will by no means leave the guilty unpunished . . . (Nahum 1:3).

Chapter 2

The Relentless Persecution of the Jews

When Moses warned the Children of Israel that their greatest punishment for disobedience would be ejection from their Promised Land, he also told them that wherever they went in the world, they would be persecuted.

As recorded in Leviticus, Moses said that if their persistent sin led to their worldwide dispersion, God would "draw out a sword" after them (Leviticus 26:33). He further stated that God would "bring weakness into their hearts in the lands of their enemies" and that "the sound of a driven leaf" would cause them fear (Leviticus 26:36).

In the same speech, as recorded in Deuteronomy 28, Moses described in even more graphic language the horrible fate of relentless persecution that they would experience if they were ejected from their land and scattered worldwide:

> 65) "Among those nations you shall find no rest, and there will be no resting place for the sole of your foot; but there the LORD will give you a trembling heart, failing of eyes, and despair of soul.
>
> 66) "So your life shall hang in doubt before you; and you will be in dread night and day, and shall have no assurance of your life.

> 67) "In the morning you shall say, 'Would that it were evening!' And at evening you shall say, 'Would that it were morning!' because of the dread of your heart which you dread, and for the sight of your eyes which you will see.

Tragically, the warnings in all these prophecies came true as the Jewish people persisted in their rebellion against God and were ultimately dispersed from their land worldwide, where they experienced constant persecution.

And even more tragic is the fact that most of that persecution came from professing Christians who were advocates of what came to be known as "Replacement Theology."

The Theology of Anti-Semitism

For almost 2,000 years the Church at large, both Catholic and Protestant, has maintained that due to the fact the Jews rejected Jesus as their Messiah, God poured out His wrath on them in 70 AD, destroying their nation and their temple, and that He has washed His hands of them, leaving them with no purpose whatsoever as a nation..

In short, because of their rebellion against God in their rejection of Jesus, God has replaced Israel with the Church, transferring the blessings promised to Israel to the Church.

This is called "Replacement Theology," and those who believe in it constitute the majority of professing Christians today.[1] Accordingly, they consider modern day Israel to be an accident of history, with no spiritual significance whatsoever.

And therefore, they would deny that God has any special plans for the Jewish people in the end times. Again, to them, the regathering of the Jews and the re-establishment of Israel are simply accidents of history, with no spiritual significance.

The Origin of Replacement Theology

The roots of Replacement Theology and its fruit of anti-Semitism go back to the very beginning of Christianity. This is ironic when you consider the fact that the Church began as a Jewish institution. It was founded in Judea by Jews who were followers of a Jewish Messiah, and all its founding documents were written by Jews.[2]

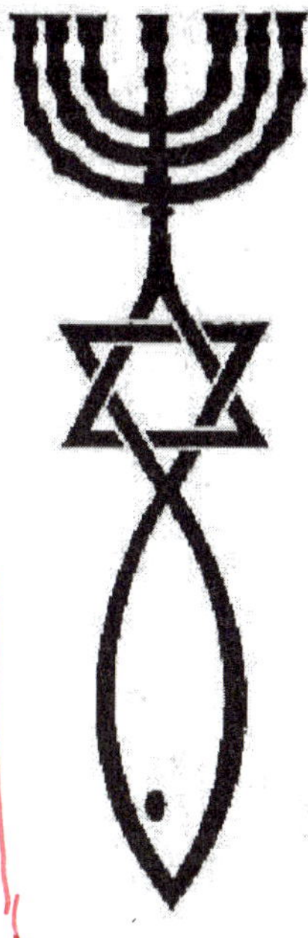

The symbol on the right is the oldest Christian symbol that has ever been found. It clearly emphasizes the Jewish origins of Christianity. The symbol is carved into artifacts found in Jerusalem that date back to the First Century.[3]

As you can see, it shows the fish, the symbol of the Church, emerging from Jewish roots, represented by the Menorah and the Star of David. The fish became a symbol for Christians because the word for fish in Greek is *icthus*, and Christians used the letters of this word, ICTHUS, as an acronym for Iesous, Christos, Theos, Huios, and Soter, meaning Jesus Christ, God's Son and Savior.

But the distinctive Jewish flavor of early Christianity was not to last long. As the Church began to spread beyond Judea, its message was embraced by more and more Gentiles who had no interest in maintaining contact with the Church's Jewish roots. Even worse, the new Gentile leaders began to turn against the Jews by characterizing them as "Christ killers."

Consider the following examples:[4]

Ignatius of Antioch (ca. 50-117 AD) — Taught that those who partake of the Passover are partakers with those who killed Jesus.[5]

Justin Martyr (100-165 AD) — Claimed God's covenant with Israel was no longer valid and that the Gentiles had replaced the Jews.[6]

Irenaeus (ca. 130-202 AD) — Declared the Jews were disinherited from the grace of God.[7]

Tertullian (ca. 155-230 AD) — Blamed the Jews for the death of Jesus and argued they had been rejected by God.[8]

Origen (185-254 AD) — He was responsible for much anti-Semitism, all of which was based on his assertion that the Jews were responsible for killing Jesus.[9]

The Council of Elvira (305 AD in Spain) — Prohibited Christians from sharing a meal with a Jew, marrying a Jew, blessing a Jew or observing the Sabbath.[10]

The Council of Nicea (325 AD in Turkey) — Changed the celebration of the Resurrection from the Jewish Feast of First Fruits to Easter in an attempt to disassociate it from Jewish feasts. The Council stated: "For it is unbecoming beyond measure that on this holiest of festivals we should follow the customs of the Jews. Henceforth let us have nothing in common with this odious people . . ."[11]

Eusebius (ca. 265-339 AD) — Taught that the promises of Scripture were meant for the Gentiles and the curses were meant for the Jews. He further asserted that the Church was the "true Israel."[12]

John Chrysostom (ca. 349-407 AD) — Preached a series of sermons against the Jews in which he stated, "The synagogue is not only a brothel and a theater, it is also a den of robbers and lodging place for wild beasts . . . Jews are inveterate murderers possessed by the Devil. Their debauchery and drunkenness gives the manners of a pig." He denied that Jews could ever receive forgiveness. He claimed it was a Christian duty to hate Jews. He claimed that Jews worshiped Satan. And this man was canonized a saint![13]

Jerome (ca. 347-420 AD) — Described the Jews as ". . . serpents wearing the image of Judas. Their psalms and prayers are the braying of donkeys . . . They are incapable of understanding Scripture . . ."[14]

St. Augustine (354-430 AD) — Asserted that the Jews deserved death but were destined "to wander the earth to witness the victory of the Church over the synagogue."[15]

The Middle Ages

By the Middle Ages, two erroneous concepts had become established Church doctrine:

1) The Jews should be considered "Christ killers" and should be mistreated accordingly.

2) The Church has replaced Israel, and God has no future purpose for the Jews.

These concepts were reinforced throughout the Middle Ages through the Crusades, the Inquisition, passion plays, the black plague epidemic, and blood libels.

In 1095 Pope Urban II called for a crusade to rid the Holy Land of its Muslim rulers. Although the prime goal of the crusade was to liberate Jerusalem from the Muslims, Jews were a second target. The accumulated hatreds and fears resulting from charges of deicide (the murder of God) exploded with this call to arms. The Abbot of Cluny asked why Christians should travel to "the ends of the world to fight the Saracens, when we permit among us other infidels a thousand times more guilty toward Christ than the Mohammedans?" Religious passion, greed, and the vulnerability of Jews led to the rise of violent mobs who murdered thousands of Jews to the cry of "Conversion or death!" This behavior continued for eight additional crusades until the 9th in 1271-1272.[16]

Passion plays abounded during the Middle Ages, and they were used to cultivate hatred toward the Jewish people. Jews were depicted as demons who knew full well that Christ was the Son of God. In each play, as the actor portraying Christ carried the cross, he was tortured by bloodthirsty, cursing devils with hooked noses, horns and tails. The Jews were made to seem as evil as Christ was divine.[17]

Throughout the Middle Ages, professing Christians spread myths which helped to heighten popular hatred and fear of the Jewish people. As a result, it became common-place among Christian groups to think of Jews as agents of Satan. One of the most popular anti-Jewish myths that gained widespread acceptance was the notion that Jews murdered Christians each year around the time of Passover in order to get blood needed to perform satanic rites. This became known as the charge of ritual murder or "blood libel." Another common myth that circulated during these years was that Jews would steal the wafers used in communion and stab them with knives, thus killing Christ once again![18]

The Black Plague in the middle of the fourteenth century killed approximately one-third of the population of Europe. At the time, it was not known how the illness spread, but stories and rumors circulated that Jews had poisoned the wells. Although the accusation was totally unfounded, many Christians believed the myth. One reason it was easy to believe is because the Jews were not impacted by the plague as much as were the Gentiles. But this was due to the sanitary laws of the Bible which the Jews carefully followed. This accusation led to severe consequences for Jews. More than sixty Jewish communities were burned to the ground with all their occupants killed, and in some places, Jews were tortured and burned to death in bonfires.[19]

In 1478, Pope Sixtus IV granted the monarchs of Spain, Ferdinand and Isabella, the right to establish a special inquisition in Spain to deal with baptized Jews who were suspected of remaining faithful to Judaism. Thousands were burned at the stake by order of the Spanish Inquisition. In 1492, King Ferdinand decided that all Spanish Jews should be banned from Spain. It was feared that Jews were a danger to Christianity. Approximately 150,000 Jews were forced to leave Spain.[20]

The Impact of the Reformation

Unfortunately, the Reformation produced no changes in attitude. In fact, the hatred of the Jews was reinforced and intensified by the writings of Martin Luther, the very man who launched the Reformation.

Initially, Luther was sympathetic toward the Jews because he believed their rejection of the Gospel was due to their recognition of the corruption of the Roman Catholic Church.

But when they continued to reject the Gospel, Luther turned on them with a vengeance. In 1543 he wrote a pamphlet entitled "On The Jews and Their Lies." The document was an anti-Semitic diatribe. In it, he referred to the Jews as:[21]

- "A miserable and accursed people"
- "Stupid fools"
- "Miserable, blind and senseless"
- "Thieves and robbers"
- "The great vermin of humanity"
- "Lazy rogues"
- "Blind and venomous"

Having dehumanized and demonized them, Luther then proceeded to make some startling proposals for dealing with them:

1) Their synagogues and schools should be burned.

2) Their houses should be destroyed.

3) Their Talmudic writings should be confiscated.

4) Their Rabbis should be forbidden to teach.

5) Their money should be taken from them.

6) They should be compelled into forced labor.

Needless to say, the Nazis gleefully quoted Luther as they rose to power and launched the Holocaust. In his book *Mein Kampf*, published in 1925, Adolf Hitler referred to Martin Luther as "a great warrior, a true statesman, and a great reformer." Keep in mind that Hitler was a professed Christian.

In 1924 at a Christian gathering in Berlin, Hitler spoke to thousands and received a standing ovation when he made the following proclamation: "I believe that today I am acting in accordance with the will of Almighty God as I announce the most important work that Christians could undertake — and that is to be against the Jews and get rid of them once and for all."[22]

Hitler then proceeded to talk about the influence of Luther on his life:[23]

> Martin Luther has been the greatest encouragement of my life. Luther was a great man. He was a giant. With one blow he heralded the coming of the new dawn and the new age. He saw clearly that the Jews need to be destroyed, and we're only beginning to see that we need to carry this work on.

At the Nuremberg trials after World War II, the Nazi leader, Julius Streicher, defended himself by saying, "I have never said anything that Martin Luther did not say."[24]

The terrible truth that Christians do not like to face, and which many are unaware of, is that the Holocaust was the product of 1,900 years of virulent Christian anti-Semitism.

The New Anti-Semitism

The horror of the Holocaust tended to mute the most radical forms of anti-Semitism among Christian leaders. But in reality, anti-Semitism continues today in a new sophisticated form called anti-Zionism. Whereas anti-Semitism sought to drive out the Jews from the lands where they lived, anti-Zionism refuses to accept their right to live in their own land.

A good example of the new anti-Semitism can be found in a document issued by Dr. James Kennedy's Knox Theological Seminary in 2002. It took the form of an open letter to Evangelicals concerning the land of Israel.[25] It has since been endorsed by hundreds of theologians and pastors, including such luminaries as R. C. Sproul.

The document begins by denouncing those who teach that the Bible's promises concerning the land of Israel are being fulfilled today "in a special region or 'Holy Land,' perpetually set apart by God for one ethnic group alone."[26] It then proceeds to proclaim that the promises made to Abraham "do not apply to any particular ethnic group, but to the church of Jesus Christ, ***the true Israel***" (emphasis added).[27]

The document then specifically denies the Jew's claim on any land in the Middle East: "The entitlement of any one ethnic or religious group to territory in the Middle East called the 'Holy Land' cannot be supported by Scripture." Then, incredibly, the document asserts that "the land promises specific to Israel in the Old Testament were fulfilled under Joshua."[28]

Adding salt to the wounds, the document concludes with the following observation:[29]

> The present secular state of Israel . . . is not an authentic or prophetic realization of the Messianic kingdom of Jesus Christ. Furthermore, a day should not be anticipated in which Christ's kingdom will manifest Jewish distinctives, whether by its location in "the land," by its constituency, or by its ceremonial institutions and practices.

And so you have it — an overview of the sad and sordid history of Christian anti-Semitism that is rooted in Replacement Theology and which continues to this day under the guise of anti-Zionism.

The Jewish Attitude

I hope now you can understand why it is so difficult to share the Gospel with Jews. Because Jews have been persecuted and killed throughout history in the name of Jesus, the Jewish people look upon Christianity as their mortal enemy.

Any Jew who converts to Christianity is considered a traitor, for he is viewed as one who has joined the enemy. That's the reason that Orthodox Jews react so strongly to a child who becomes a Christian. They will sometimes declare the child to be dead and will even conduct a funeral service.

This is the reason that the Messianic Jewish Movement today is such a miracle. Beginning only in 1971, it has successfully shared the Gospel with millions of Jews worldwide and has established over 800 Messianic congregations around the globe.[30]

The Response of Scripture

What does the Word of God have to say about all this? To begin with, it strongly repudiates anti-Semitism. Psalm 129:5-8 says that "all who hate Zion" will be "put to shame . . ." It further states that no believer should ever give a blessing to such a person.

With regard to the allegation that the Jews are "Christ killers," the Word clearly identifies who murdered Jesus and makes it plain that they were not exclusively the Jews. In Acts 4:27 we are told that Jesus was killed through a conspiracy that involved "both Herod and Pontius Pilate, along with the Gentiles and the peoples of Israel." In reality, all of us have the blood of Jesus on our hands, for all of us have sinned (Romans 3:23), and Jesus died for all sinners (1 Corinthians 15:3).

Regarding the idea that God has already fulfilled the land promises to the Jews during the time of Joshua, it is interesting to note that long after Joshua, David wrote a psalm stating that the land promise is everlasting in nature and is yet to be fulfilled (Psalm 105:8-11). The fact of the matter is that the Jews have never occupied all the land that was promised to them in the Abrahamic Covenant (Genesis 15:18-21).

Concerning the claim that the Jews have been rejected by God, there are a couple of biblical principles that need to be kept in mind. First, the Bible affirms that the Jews were called as God's Chosen People to be witnesses of what it means to have a relationship with Him (Isaiah 43:10-12). And the Bible makes it clear that this calling is "irrevocable" (Romans 11:29).

Second, in direct contradiction of Replacement Theology, the Bible teaches that the Jews have never been rejected by God because of their unbelief. In Romans 3 Paul asserts point blank that their rejection of Jesus has not nullified God's faithfulness to the promises He has made to them (Romans 3:1-4). Paul makes the point again in Romans 11:1 when he asks, "I say then, God has not rejected His people, has He?" He answers his own question with an emphatic statement: "May it never be! . . . God has not rejected His people whom He foreknew" (Romans 11:2).

It is true that the Jewish people are currently under discipline because of their rejection of their Messiah. Over and over in the Hebrew Scriptures the prophets said they would be disciplined if they were unfaithful, but always the promise was made that they would be preserved. An example of this type of prophetic statement can be found in Jeremiah 30:11:

> "For I am with you," declares the Lord, "to save you; for I will destroy completely all the nations where I have scattered you, only I will not destroy you completely. But I will chasten you justly, and will by no means leave you unpunished."

God has preserved them in His grace because He loves them. In Zechariah 2:8 God proclaims that the Jewish people are "the apple of His eye," and He warns against anyone trying to harm them.

Another reason they have been preserved is because God is determined to bring a great remnant to salvation (Isaiah 10:20-22). This promise is made repeatedly throughout the Hebrew Scriptures and is confirmed by Paul in the New Testament in Romans 9-11. The salvation of this remnant is described in detail in Zechariah 12:10 where it says that at the end of the Tribulation the remaining Jews will come to the end of themselves and will turn their hearts to God in repentance and accept Yeshua as their Messiah.

That believing remnant will go into the Millennium in the flesh and will comprise the nation of Israel to whom God will fulfill all the promises He has made to the Jews (Isaiah 60-62). During the Millennium the nation of Israel will be the prime nation in the world through whom God will bless all the other nations (Zechariah 8:22-23).

In summary, the Word of God makes it clear that Israel definitely has a role and a future in the end times.

Crucial Questions

The first question most people usually ask in response to these biblical points about Israel in the end times is this: "Why would God continue to pursue such a stubborn and rebellious people?"

The answer is that they are witnesses of God, and through them God is demonstrating His unfathomable grace. Only a God of grace would put up with them! But that is true of you and me as well. God is not doing one thing for the Jewish people that He is not willing to do for all of us. He pursues us in love despite our sinfulness, and regardless of how stiff-necked we may be, He never washes His hands of us.

This brings us to two more questions: "What is God's plan for the Jews in the end times and how will He bring about the salvation of a great remnant of them?" These questions will be answered in Part 3 of this book.

The Perseverance of Anti-Semitism

A perversion of Christianity has been the source of most anti-Semitism in the Western world. But throughout northern Africa, the Middle East, and parts of Asia, anti-Semitism has been promoted by Islam. The Qur'an calls Jews "the children of monkeys and pigs."[31]

But there are anti-Semites in this world who are neither Christian or Muslim and who have never even met a Jew. For example, several years ago, five of the top ten best selling books in Japan were virulently anti-Semitic, blaming all the problems of Japan on an "international Jewish conspiracy."[32]

Why is anti-Semitism so widespread, so persistent, so virulent, and so irrational? It's because it is fundamentally a supernatural phenomenon.

Satan hates the Jews with a passion. He hates them because God provided both the Bible and the Messiah through them. He hates them because God called them to be His Chosen People. He hates them because God has promised to save a great remnant of them. He hates them because God loves them.

The result is that he works overtime to plant seeds of hatred in people's hearts toward the Jews. He is determined to destroy every Jew on planet earth so that God cannot keep His promise to save a great remnant. He tried to annihilate them in the Holocaust. He failed. He will try to destroy them once again during the last half of the Tribulation. He will fail again.

Conclusion

God is in control, not Satan. God has the wisdom and power to orchestrate all the evil of Satan and Mankind to the triumph of His perfect will in history.

The Jews will be preserved. A great remnant will be saved. All the promises to the Jews will be fulfilled. One of those promises is found in a letter that Jeremiah wrote to the Jewish people when they were in Babylonian captivity (Jeremiah 29:11-13):

> 11) "For I know the plans that I have for you," declares the LORD, "plans for welfare and not for calamity to give you a future and a hope.
>
> 12) "Then you will call upon Me and come and pray to Me, and I will listen to you.
>
> 13) "You will seek Me and find Me when you search for Me with all your heart."

And when will this take place? Jeremiah proceeded to declare that this glorious promise would be fulfilled after the Jews are regathered to their homeland from "all the nations and from all the places where I have driven you" (Jeremiah 29:14).

Chapter 5 will tell the story of the fulfillment of that promise with the regathering of the Jewish people in unbelief from the four corners of the world.

But first, we must take a look at the fourth prophecy concerning Israel which God fulfilled before the beginning of the 20th Century.

Chapter 3

The Miraculous Preservation of the Jews

One of my spiritual mentors when I was in my 20s was a great man of God named Carl Ketcherside (1908-1989). I heard him in a question and answer session one time when he was asked, "What do you think is the greatest evidence that the Bible came from God?"

His answer: "The Yellow Pages of the phone book." Needless to say, we were all stunned by this response.

When the questioner followed-up by asking what he meant, Carl said, "Look at the names of the banks, the names of the department stores, the names of lawyers and doctors and accountants. You will see one Jewish name after another. God promised He would preserve the Jewish people, and He has."

In like manner, over 300 years ago, King Louis XIV of France (1638-1715) asked Blaise Pascal (1623-1662), the great Christian philosopher, to give him proof of the existence of God. Pascal answered, "Why the Jews, your Majesty, the Jews!"[1]

Both Ketcherside and Pascal were referring to the fulfillment of Bible prophecies about the Jews, one of the most remarkable being that despite their worldwide dispersion and unparalleled persecution, they would keep their identity and be preserved as a recognizable nation of people.

A Great Miracle

The preservation of the Jews has to be one of the greatest miracles of history. It is so remarkable — so historically stunning — that its uniqueness has been noted and commented on by a great variety of people.

Consider, for example, the great historian Arnold Toynbee (1889-1975). He fully recognized the unusual nature of the Jewish experience. In his twelve volume work, *A Study of History* (1934-1961), he traced the rise and fall of 19 major civilizations, developing a scheme of history which the Jewish civilization did not fit.

Toynbee ended up classifying the Jews as "fossils of history" because they seemed to be frozen in time, refusing to assimilate into the soup of humanity.[2]

Thomas Newton (1704-1782), the renowned British cleric and Bible scholar who served as Bishop of Bristol, declared in one of his sermons:[3]

> The preservation of the Jews is really one of the most single and illustrious acts of divine Providence . . . and what but a supernatural power could have preserved them in such a manner as none other nation upon earth hath been preserved.
>
> Nor is the providence of God less remarkable in the destruction of their enemies, than in their preservation . . . We see that the great empires, which in their turn subdued and oppressed the people of God, are all come to ruin . . . And if such hath been the fatal end of the enemies and oppressors of the Jews, let it serve as a warning to all those, who at any time or upon any occasion are for raising a clamor and persecution against them.

Leo Tolstoy (1828-1910), the great Russian novelist, expressed his awe over the preservation of the Jews with these words:[4]

> What is the Jew? . . . What kind of unique creature is this whom all the rulers of all the nations of the world have disgraced and crushed and expelled . . . persecuted, burned and drowned, and who, despite their anger and fury, continue to live and to flourish . . . The Jew is the symbol of eternity.

To get a feel for how preposterous the preservation of the Jews is from a human perspective, consider this illustration by Rabbi Dov Greenberg who is the Executive Director of Chabad (the Jewish Hasidic Movement) at Stanford University:[5]

> Imagine we could travel back in time and say to the great Pharaoh [of Moses' time], "There is good news and bad news. The good news is that one of the nations alive today will survive and change the moral landscape of the world. The bad news is: it won't be yours. It will be that group of Hebrew slaves out there, building your glorious temples, the Children of Israel."

> Nothing would sound more outrageous. The Egypt of Pharaoh's time was the greatest empire of the ancient world, brilliant in arts and sciences, formidable in war. The Israelites were a landless people, powerless slaves. Indeed, already in antiquity, those in power believed that the Israelites were on the verge of extinction.

Perhaps the most insightful commentary on the immortality of the Jewish people was written by the American novelist

Mark Twain (1835-1910) who was an agnostic and a skeptic. His article appeared in Harper's magazine in 1899:[6]

> If the statistics are right, the Jews constitute but one quarter of one percent of the human race. It suggests a nebulous dim puff of stardust lost in the blaze of the Milky Way.
>
> Properly, the Jew ought hardly to be heard of, but he is heard of, has always been heard of. He is as prominent on the planet as any other people, and his importance is extravagantly out of proportion to the smallness of his bulk.
>
> His contributions to the world's list of great names in literature, science, art, music, finance, medicine and abstruse learning are very out of proportion to the weakness of his numbers. He has made a marvelous fight in this world in all ages; and has done it with his hands tied behind him. He could be vain of himself and be excused for it.
>
> The Egyptians, the Babylonians and the Persians rose, filled the planet with sound and splendor; then faded to dream-stuff and passed away; the Greeks and the Romans followed and made a vast noise, and they are gone; other peoples have sprung up and held their torch high for a time but it burned out, and they sit in twilight now, or have vanished.
>
> The Jew saw them all, survived them all, and is now what he always was, exhibiting no decadence, no infirmities of age, no weakening of his parts, no slowing of his energies, no dulling of his alert and aggressive mind. All things are mortal but the Jew; all other forces

> pass, but he remains. What is the secret of his immortality?

Twain's question, "What is the secret of his immortality?" can be answered in only one way, and that answer was provided by David Ben-Gurion (1886-1973), the first Prime Minister of Israel: "In Israel, in order to be a realist, you must believe in miracles."[7]

The Magnitude of the Miracle

The preservation of the Jewish people throughout their 2,700 years of dispersion is mind-boggling. Keep in mind that they were dispersed to over 130 nations worldwide, and they were brutally mistreated wherever they went. Will Varner, a professor at The Master's College, has expressed it this way: "No nation in the history of the world ever has been exiled from its land, lost its national existence and language, and then returned as a people to that identical homeland and even revived its ancient tongue. No nation, that is, except one — the nation of Israel."[8]

The relentless persecution of the Jews dates from the very beginning of their existence as a nation. The Pharaoh of Egypt attempted to murder all their male babies (Exodus 1:15-16). A government bureaucrat named Haman conceived a genocidal plan to exterminate all the Jewish people in Persia (Esther 3:8-10). The Assyrian Empire conquered ten of the Jewish tribes and scattered them throughout Asia. Then came the Babylonian exile of the remaining two tribes and the two horrific wars with the Romans (70 and 135 AD).

Throughout the Middle Ages, the Jews were herded into ghettos and required to wear identifying symbols. They were subjected to pogroms, witch hunts, and blood libels. They were blamed for all the problems of society — even for the Black Plague. They were slaughtered during the Crusades, they were tortured during the Inquisition, and they became an object of complete annihilation during the Nazi Holocaust.[9]

Yet, the Jewish people survived and their persecutors ended up in the dust bin of history.

How could this be? Chance? Coincidence? Good luck? A roll of the dice? There are many theories.

Secular Theories

The most common theory offered by secular Jews is that the overwhelming persecution suffered by the Jewish people created within them an iron will to survive, and their genius as a people produced cunning and crafty methods of survival.[10] But all such naturalistic explanations seem shallow and fall flat in the face of the odds that any people could preserve their existence and identity in the midst of so much suffering.

Other secular arguments include the high degree of education and literacy that characterized the Jews during the Middle Ages. This enabled them to more effectively preserve their traditions, and it increased their usefulness to society.[11] Instead of living as beggars, they were able to become lawyers, doctors, bankers and bureaucrats.

Their high level of education also made it possible for them to be extremely mobile, enabling them to move more easily from one nation to another. They had financial resources, and they posed less of a welfare problem than non-Jewish migrants.[12]

Religious Theories

I'm sure all these elements were significant, but religious Jewish spokesmen have done much better with their explanation of Jewish survival. As one rabbi has put it: "The supernatural element of Jewish survival must be squarely faced."[13] Another rabbi has put it this way:[14]

> If we wish to discover the essential elements making up the . . . unique strength [of

> the Jewish people], we must conclude that it is not its peculiar physical or intrinsic mental characteristics, nor its tongue, manners and customs . . . The only link which unites our scattered people throughout its dispersion, regardless of time, is Torah and mitzvot.

Torah and mitzvot — these two are the focus of Orthodox Jewish explanations of the preservation of the Jewish people. Torah refers to the first five books of the Hebrew Scriptures — the books written by Moses, often referred to as the Pentateuch. Mitzvot are the commandments contained in the Torah.

The rabbis contend that there are 613 mitzvot in the Torah.[15] They view 248 of these commandments as positive in nature ("thou shalt"). The remaining total of 365 are considered to be negative ("thou shalt not"). All the commandments are viewed as essential for a person to be holy as God is holy (Leviticus 20:26).

The problem is that all the mitzvot must be interpreted as to their daily application, a process that results in endless discussions and disputes and often conflicting conclusions. An example would be the commandment against building a fire on the Sabbath (Exodus 35:3). The commandment is clear enough. But, does flipping a light switch or pushing an elevator button constitute the striking of a fire?

Halacha

Over the centuries, the Jewish sages have developed an extensive code of oral laws that apply the mitzvot of the Torah to every aspect of daily life. This code is called Halacha.[16] It is often referred to as "Jewish Law." But a more literal translation would be "the way to behave" or "the way of walking."

The observance of Halacha within the Diaspora during the 2,000 years since the destruction of the Jewish Temple in 70 AD prevented the Jewish people from becoming assimilated into the cultures where they were dispersed. The practice of Halacha enabled them to keep their identity as a people set apart by God to be a witness to the world (Deuteronomy 7:6-8).

One rabbi has referred to observance of Halacha as "the tenacious adherence to our spiritual heritage."[17] He has further stated "We [the Jewish people] are who and what we are because of a momentous faith, a faith that proved stronger than the greatest empires in history."[18]

Rabbi Akiva (50-137 AD), the great Jewish sage of the Second Century, resorted to the following illustration to explain why the Jewish people must reject assimilation at all costs:[19]

> A fox was once walking by the bank of a river, and saw fish darting from place to place. "What are you fleeing from?" he asked the fish. "To escape the nets of the fisherman." "In that case," said the fox, "come and live on dry land together with me." "Are you the one they describe as the cleverest of animals?" the fish replied. "You are not clever but foolish. If we are in danger here in the water, which is where we live, how much more so on dry land, where we are bound to die."

Explaining the illustration, Rabbi Akiva stressed that the Torah is to Jewish survival as water is to a fish. Yes, the Jews are in constant danger, but if they put the Torah aside, they will lose their identity and die out as an identifiable people.

The Power of Memory

Another key element to keeping their identity which is often stressed in rabbinical writings is memory. Thus, all the

Jewish feast days are reminders of either great events in Jewish history or promises of God about the future, or both.[20]

For example, the Feast of Passover points the Jewish memory back to the time when God miraculously delivered the Jews from Egyptian captivity. The Feast of Shavu'ot (known to Christians as the Feast of Pentecost) is a reminder of the giving of the Law to Moses on Mount Sinai. The most joyous feast of the year is the Feast of Tabernacles (Sukkot in Hebrew) in the Fall of the year. It celebrates the completion of the fruit harvest, and it serves as a reminder of how God was faithful to the Jews during their wilderness wanderings when they lived in tabernacles. It is also a reminder that God has promised in His Word that one day He will come to the earth to tabernacle among His people (Zechariah 2:10-13).

The observance of the seven Jewish feasts each year — year after year — kept alive in Jewish hearts the memory of God's call on their life as a nation. They were reminded of how God had come to their rescue time and time again (Psalm 78) and how He had promised that one day they would become the prime nation in the world, through whom all of God's blessings would flow to the nations (Isaiah 2:1-4).

A Problem

The problem with these explanations of Jewish preservation is that they only show how the Jews kept their identity — and not how they were able to survive. As a matter of fact, the maintenance of their unique identity made them an object of hatred and an easy target for abuse.

The result was 2,000 years of unrelenting hatred, persecution and slaughter. Their own Scriptures prophesied that once they were scattered, they would be persecuted wherever they went and would become few in number:

> And the LORD will scatter you among the peoples, and you shall be left few in number

> among the nations, where the LORD shall drive you (Deuteronomy 4:27).
>
> Then [after their scattering] you shall be left few in number, whereas you were as numerous as the stars of heaven, because you did not obey the LORD your God (Deuteronomy 28: 62).

Roman records indicate that 2,000 years ago there were between 8 to 10 million Jews living in the world.[21] There are 14 million today. How many should there be?

Well, as I pointed out in chapter 1, in the same period of time, the population of China grew from 30 million to over one billion.[22] The Arab peoples came into existence at the same time as the Jews. Today there are more than 350 million Arabs.[23] Based on these statistics, the Jewish population today should be between 400 and 500 million.

Back to the Basic Question

So, we find ourselves still grappling with the question we began with: "How did the Jews survive?" And there is really only one answer: "Supernaturally." Psalm 124 sums it up best:

> 1) "Had it not been the LORD who was on our side," let Israel now say,
>
> 2) "Had it not been the LORD who was on our side when men rose up against us,
>
> 3) Then they would have swallowed us alive, when their anger was kindled against us;
>
> 4) Then the waters would have engulfed us, the stream would have swept over our soul;
>
> 5) Then the raging waters would have swept over our soul."

> 6) Blessed be the LORD, who has not given us to be torn by their teeth.
>
> 7) Our soul has escaped as a bird out of the snare of the trapper; the snare is broken and we have escaped.
>
> 8) Our help is in the name of the LORD, who made heaven and earth.

Although this passage probably speaks specifically about the survival of the Children of Israel during their wilderness wanderings under the leadership of Moses, it expresses an eternal principle concerning God's relationship with the Jewish people. The author of Psalm 121 put it this way: "Behold, He who keeps Israel will neither slumber nor sleep" (Psalm 121:4).

God's Promise to Preserve His People

The Hebrew prophets were very precise about the fact that God would always preserve the Jewish people. Consider this symbolic prophecy of Isaiah who wrote 2,700 years ago, 700 years before the birth of Jesus (Isaiah 49:14-16):

> 14) But Zion [the Jewish people] said, "The LORD has forsaken me, and the Lord has forgotten me."
>
> 15) [God answers] "Can a woman forget her nursing child and have no compassion on the son of her womb? Even these may forget, but I will not forget you.
>
> 16) "Behold, I have inscribed you on the palms of My hands . . ."

Speaking more specifically, Isaiah wrote these words about the preservation of the Jews (Isaiah 41:10-11):

> 10) "Do not fear, for I am with you; do not anxiously look about you, for I am your God. I will strengthen you, surely I will help you, surely I will uphold you with My righteous right hand.
>
> 11) "Behold, all those who are angered at you will be shamed and dishonored; those who contend with you will be as nothing and will perish."

Likewise, the prophet Jeremiah, who wrote 75 years after Isaiah, declared that God would preserve the Jewish people (Jeremiah 30:11):

> "For I am with you," declares the LORD, "to save you; for I will destroy completely all the nations where I have scattered you, only I will not destroy you completely. But I will chasten you justly and will by no means leave you unpunished."

A more graphic prophecy by Jeremiah concerning the preservation of the Jews can be found in Jeremiah 31 —

> 35) Thus says the LORD, who gives the sun for light by day and the fixed order of the moon and the stars for light by night, who stirs up the sea so that its waves roar; the LORD of hosts is His name:
>
> 36) "If this fixed order departs from before Me," declares the LORD, "Then the offspring of Israel also will cease from being a nation before Me forever."
>
> 37) Thus says the LORD, "If the heavens above can be measured and the foundations of the earth searched out below, then I will also cast off all the offspring of Israel for all that

they have done," declares the LORD.

The Permanence of the Jews

So, when will the Jewish people cease to exist? When the sun stops coming up and going down, when the seasons of the year cease to come, and only after all the heavens and the depths of the oceans have been explored. In short, the Jewish people are here to stay.

Do I need to inform you that these prophecies have been fulfilled? Despite their dispersion, their persecution and the murderous pogroms leading up to the Holocaust, 6.5 million Jews live in Israel today (slightly more than the number killed in the Holocaust), with another 7.5 million in other countries.

Now, you can understand why the continuing existence of the Jewish people is proof positive that there is a God and that the Bible is His Word.

Before continuing with the story of the Jewish people in Bible prophecy, we must pause to consider a very important prophecy that God gave to them about their land.

Chapter 4

The Desolation of the Land of Israel

Before the children of Israel entered the Promised Land, God spoke a series of stern warnings to them through Moses, their leader and prophet. The warnings are recorded in Deuteronomy 28 and 29.

These chapters constitute God's Land Covenant with the Jewish people. In this covenant, God made it clear that although He had given the Jewish people an everlasting title to the land, their enjoyment of it would depend on their obedience to the laws He had given them in the Mosaic Covenant.

The Hope of Blessings

The Land Covenant begins with promises of blessings if they are obedient (Deuteronomy 28:1-2):

> 1) "Now it shall be, if you diligently obey the LORD your God, being careful to do all His commandments which I command you today, the LORD your God will set you high above all the nations of the earth.
>
> 2) "All these blessings will come upon you and overtake you if you obey the LORD your God . . ."

Moses then proceeded to enumerate the blessings in detail. They included such things as agricultural abundance, defeat of enemies, financial prosperity and abundant rain (Deuteronomy 28:3-13).

The Warning of Curses

But then, Moses started issuing warnings about curses that would come upon them if they were disobedient to the Lord (Deuteronomy 28:15ff). The variety of these curses was breathtaking — cities in chaos, youth in rebellion, an epidemic of divorce, confusing governmental policies, defeats by their enemies, rampant disease, drought leading to crop failures, foreign domination and even exile to a foreign land.

Moses concluded the list with a detailed explanation of what would be the ultimate judgment of God should they become entrenched in rebellion and refuse to repent (Deuteronomy 28:64-67):

> 64) "Moreover, the LORD will scatter you among all peoples, from one end of the earth to the other end of the earth; and there you shall serve other gods, wood and stone, which you or your fathers have not known.
>
> 65) "Among those nations you shall find no rest, and there will be no resting place for the sole of your foot; but there the LORD will give you a trembling heart, failing of eyes, and despair of soul.
>
> 66) "So your life shall hang in doubt before you; and you will be in dread night and day, and shall have no assurance of your life.
>
> 67) "In the morning you shall say, 'Would that it were evening!' And at evening you shall say, 'Would that it were morning!' because of the dread of your heart which you dread, and for the sight of your eyes which you will see."

In summary, the ultimate punishment the Jewish people would receive for willful and unrepentant rebellion against God's Word would be ejection from their land, their scattering worldwide, and their persecution wherever they went.

The Curse on the Land

Nor would that be all. Moses further stated that God would put a curse on their land, and as a result of that curse, the land would become filled with diseases and plagues (Deuteronomy 29:22). The land itself would become "a burning waste, unsown and unproductive, and no grass [growing] in it . . ." (Deuteronomy 29:23).

The curse would be so terrible that when foreigners came to visit the land, they would cry out, "Why has the LORD done this to the land? Why this great outburst of anger?" (Deuteronomy 29:24).

And the answer will be: "Because they forsook the covenant of the LORD, the God of their fathers . . . [and] they went and served other gods and worshiped them . . . Therefore, the anger of the LORD burned against that land, to bring upon it every curse which is written in this book; and the LORD uprooted them from their land in anger and in fury and in great wrath . . ." (Deuteronomy 29:25-28).

The Promise of Hope

Fortunately for the Jewish people, Moses did not leave it there. He continued on to speak some words of hope. He assured them that if they were ever scattered all over the world, a day would come when God in His compassion would "restore them from captivity" by regathering them to their homeland (Deuteronomy 30:3). "If your outcasts are at the ends of the earth, from there the LORD your God will gather you, and from there He will bring you back" (Deuteronomy 30:4).

The prophet Ezekiel picked it up from there, prophesying what would happen to the land when the Jewish people were regathered to it (Ezekiel 36:34-35):

> 34) The desolate land will be cultivated instead of being a desolation in the sight of everyone who passes by.
>
> 35) They will say, "This desolate land has become like the garden of Eden; and the waste, desolate and ruined cities are fortified and inhabited."

Prophetic Fulfillment

What an incredible panorama of future events that have been fulfilled precisely in detail!

After the Jewish people occupied their Promised Land under the leadership of Joshua, they immediately began to stray from God's Word. They violated God's command not to intermarry with the pagan peoples of the land. As they did so, they began to worship the false gods of these peoples.

God responded by sending prophets to call them to repentance. When they refused to repent, God began to afflict them with the very curses that Moses had outlined in his warnings. Finally, just as Moses had prophesied, they were taken into exile, first the northern kingdom of Israel (722 BC) and then the southern kingdom of Judah (586 BC).

After God allowed the Jews of the southern kingdom to return from their Babylonian captivity, they persisted in their rebellion, consummating with the rejection of the Messiah whom God had sent to them.

It was at that point that God allowed the Romans to destroy Jerusalem in 70 AD, including the Jewish Temple. This resulted in their ejection from the land and their worldwide scattering, a process that was accelerated after the Second

Jewish Revolt in 132-136 AD.

Over the next 1800 years the Jews were literally scattered to the four corners of the earth, in fulfillment of Moses' prophecy. And in further fulfillment of prophecy, they were persecuted wherever they went, and their homeland became utterly desolate.

The Nature of the Promised Land

Keep in mind that their homeland was one of great abundance when the Jewish people entered it some 1400 years before the time of Jesus. Here's how it was described by Moses (Deuteronomy 8:7-9):

> 7) ". . . the LORD your God is bringing you into a good land, a land of brooks of water, of fountains and springs, flowing forth in valleys and hills;
>
> 8) a land of wheat and barley, of vines and fig trees and pomegranates, a land of olive oil and honey;
>
> 9) a land where you will eat food without scarcity, in which you will not lack anything; a land whose stones are iron, and out of whose hills you can dig copper."

Moses further characterized the land as being very different from the arid land of Egypt because it "drinks from the rain of heaven" (Deuteronomy 11:10-11). Moses also described it as "a land for which the LORD your God cares; the eyes of the LORD your God are always on it, from the beginning even to the end of the year" (Deuteronomy 11:12).

Ezekiel affirmed this evaluation of the land many years later when he wrote that God swore to the Jewish people that He would bring them out of the land of Egypt into a land "flowing with milk and honey, which is the glory of all lands"

(Ezekiel 20:6-7,15).

The Desolation of the Land

Yet, just as prophesied, this glorious land became "a haunt of jackals" and "a heap of ruins" (Jeremiah 9:11).

Rainfall diminished, trees were cut down, top soil eroded and excessive sedimentation in the valleys resulted in water-logging and the creation of swamps. With swamps came an outbreak of malaria which weakened the population and led to the abandonment of villages and formerly cultivated land.[1]

The land became repugnant, and during the 1800 years the Jews were exiled from it, no one really desired it. It became a deserted wasteland, and Jerusalem became an incubator of disease. By the beginning of the 19th Century, it was a place people avoided, except for the most fanatical Christian pilgrims — like the Russians who would walk all the way to the Holy Land and die there.

In my library I have a number of books written in the 19th Century by Western explorers who wrote graphic descriptions of the land. Following are some examples.

1855

In 1855 an American medical doctor named Jonathan Miesse traveled to the Holy Land and published his recollections in 1859 in a book titled *A Journey to Egypt and Palestine*.[2] (Israel had been renamed Palestine by the Romans and was still called by that name in the 19th Century). Dr. Miesse wrote:[3]

> . . . at present, nearly three thousand years after David, the country is a prey to the wild beasts, and to the wilder Bedouins; and of the inhabitants, each plants just enough to satisfy his greatest bodily wants, all surplus the Bedouin will take, and what he leaves behind, the ruling Turk will confiscate.

His reference to the Turks pointed to another curse on the land. The Ottoman Empire of the Turks had taken control of the land in 1516, and they quickly established a reputation for administrative incompetence and corruption.

1867

Twelve years later, Mark Twain made a trip to Palestine. He was a journalist at the time for a San Francisco newspaper. He published his impressions in 1869 in a book titled *The Innocents Abroad*.[4] It was the book that made Twain famous. He described Palestine as a "blistering, naked, treeless land."[5]

Regarding the Sea of Galilee area, in particular, Twain wrote, "There is not a solitary village . . . There are two or three small clusters of Bedouin tents, but not a single permanent habitation. One may ride ten miles, hereabouts, and not see ten human beings." Then, referring to Bible prophecy, he wrote, "To this region, the prophecies apply: 'I will bring the land into desolation; and your enemies which dwell therein shall be astonished at it'" (Leviticus 26:32).[6]

A reference to fulfilled prophecy in this passage is remarkable since Mark Twain was not a believer. Even more so when you consider that he added this statement: "No man can stand here [in this deserted area] and say the prophecy has not been fulfilled."[7]

Concerning the Valley of Jezreel (or the Valley of Armageddon, as Christians call it), Twain observed, "A desolation is here that not even imagination can grace with the pomp of life and action."[8] He described the central highlands of Samaria by stating, "There was hardly a tree or a shrub anywhere. Even the olive and the cactus, those fast friends of a worthless soil, had almost deserted the country."[9] Continuing with his description of Samaria, he wrote: "No landscape exists that is more tiresome to the eye than that which bounds the approaches to Jerusalem."[10]

Twain's summary description of the land was a dismal one: ". . . it truly is monotonous and uninviting . . . It is a hopeless, dreary, heart-broken land."[11]

Twain concluded his observations about Palestine in the mid-19th Century with these poignant words: "Palestine sits in sackcloth and ashes . . . and why should it be otherwise? Can the curse of the Deity beautify a land?"[12]

1884

Another American tourist, Henry M. Field, published a book about his trip to Palestine in 1884. He wrote about the treeless, desolate landscape as follows:[13]

> The country seemed deserted of human habitations . . . Its appearance was made still more desolate by being without trees. While riding among the hills, I did not see a single tree. Whether this be owing to the government tax on trees, or the wastefulness of the people in cutting for fuel every young tree almost as soon as it shows its head above the ground, I know not; I only state the fact, that the landscape was absolutely treeless.

1912

As the 20th Century began and the Jews started to return to their homeland, the condition of the land had not improved. In 1912 a British traveler by the name of Sir Frederick Treves, published a book appropriately titled, "*The Land That Is Desolate*.[14]

Describing the approach to Jerusalem, Treves wrote:[15]

> It is practically treeless. Such hedges as exist are mostly of prickly cactus . . . The villages passed are secretive-looking clumps of flat-topped huts made, it would seem, of a

> chocolate-coloured mud and decorated with litter and refuse.

Speaking of the area surrounding Jerusalem, Treves observed that "the hills are bare save for some hectic grass and starveling scrub."[16] As for Jerusalem, he wrote:[17]

> . . . the city itself is as the shadow of a rock in a weary land. With the exception of a few pallid olive trees, a patch here and there of indefinite green, and a melancholy cypress, the environs of Jerusalem are a dusty, ungenial limestone waste.

Treves described Bethlehem as "a drab city of drab houses on a drab ridge, as monotonous in colour and as cheerless looking as a pile of dry bones."[18] Likewise, he wrote about the Nazareth area as being "a sorry country, for the land is bare, harsh, and treeless . . . Here is assuredly to be seen the poverty of the earth."[19] Regarding the Galilee area, he described it as "abandoned."[20] Concerning the "wholly dirty town of Tiberias," he stated that it was "a wretched and stinking place" with "sturdy vermin."[21]

1924

Even as late as the mid-1920s, Palestine was still being described as "a barren, rocky and forbidding land" by Oliver C. Dalby in his booklet, *Rambles in Scriptural Lands*.[22] He characterized Jerusalem as a place where the streets were "narrow and dirty," and where "the buildings are austere and unattractive."[23]

A Strange Miracle

In a book published in 2007, an American Orthodox Jewish Rabbi named Menachem Kohen, asserted that the greatest miracle performed by God during the past 1800 years was one that occurred daily in the land of Palestine — namely, little or no rain.[24] He refers to it as a "reoccurring miracle."[25] And he asserts that this miracle of drought was for the purpose of fulfilling prophecies in Deuteronomy 28 which read: "The LORD will make the rain of your land powder and dust . . ." (Deuteronomy 28:24). He also points to other prophecies:

> You shall bring out much seed to the field but you will gather in little, for the locust will consume it (Deuteronomy 28:38).
>
> The locust shall possess all your trees and the produce of your ground (Deuteronomy 28: 42).

Additionally, Rabbi Kohen contends that this reoccurring miracle of God was for the purpose of protecting the Jewish homeland from occupation by foreign Gentiles. In other words, God purposefully made the land desolate so that it could be preserved for the Jews when He would regather them in the end times — at which time the land would be reclaimed.[26]

A Palestinian Lie

Incredibly, today the Palestinians are claiming that the land was never desolate despite all these written testimonies and books of photographs that clearly show Palestine to be a wasteland before the beginning of the 20th Century. They are also claiming that the Jews stole the land from them when they started returning in the early 1900s.[27]

These claims are nothing but a fairy tale. The Jews did not steal any land from anyone. Although God had given them an eternal title to the land, they purchased the land that they occupied when they began returning. And the Arabs who sold them the land, laughed all the way to the bank. They thought the Jews were fools to purchase a land denuded of trees and full of malaria-infested swamps. The Arabs were, of course, unaware of the promise of God to redeem the land and make it like the Garden of Eden whenever the Jews were regathered to their homeland (Ezekiel 36:35).

Let's turn our attention now to seven remarkable prophecies about the Jewish people that were fulfilled in whole or in part during the 20th Century.

Part 2

The Present

Chapter 5

The Regathering of the Jewish People

One of the greatest examples of God's continuing love for the Jewish people can be found in the most important prophetic development of the 20th Century.

When I think back on the 20th Century and all its amazing events, I am reminded of some words found in Habakkuk 1:5. They constitute a statement made by God to the prophet:

> Look among the nations! Observe! Be astonished! Wonder! Because I am doing something in your days — You would not believe if you were told.

The 20th Century was full of momentous events that no one could have foreseen in 1900. Looking back on that century, what would you consider to be the most important event from a biblical perspective — particularly from the viewpoint of Bible prophecy?

World Wars I & II?

The Great Depression?

The advent of space travel?

The collapse of Communism?

The reunification of Europe?

The resurgence of Islam?

The answer from a biblical perspective is none of these events. The most important development of the 20th Century — more important than all of these events put together — was the worldwide regathering of the Jewish people to their homeland.

And lest you think I am exaggerating, let me prove it to you.

The Relevant Prophecies

There are many Bible prophecies concerning the regathering of the Jewish people in unbelief. In fact, their regathering in unbelief is the most prolific prophecy in the Old Testament Scriptures.

Let's take a look at three of the most important of those prophecies. The first is found in Jeremiah 16. It is mind-boggling. Read it carefully:

> 14) "Therefore behold, days are coming," declares the LORD, "when it will no longer be said, 'As the LORD lives, who brought up the sons of Israel out of the land of Egypt,'
>
> 15) but, 'As the LORD lives, who brought up the sons of Israel from the land of the north and from all the countries where He had banished them.' For I will restore them to their own land which I gave to their fathers."

This same prophecy is repeated verbatim in Jeremiah 23:7-8.

You cannot fully appreciate what is said in these verses unless you know something about Judaism. The one event that all Jews consider to be the greatest miracle in their history is the deliverance of their ancestors from Egyptian captivity under the leadership of Moses.

But this scripture passage asserts that a time will come when the Jews will look back on their history and proclaim that their regathering from the four corners of the earth — the event that began in the 1890s and continues to this day — was a greater miracle than their deliverance from Egyptian slavery. In other words The regathering in the 20th Century will eclipse the Exodus!

This means that you and I are privileged to witness one of the greatest miracles of history. And yet, the average Christian has no appreciation for what is happening because he is ignorant of Bible prophecy and he has been taught that God is finished with the Jews. Therefore, the current regathering is simply viewed as an accident of history.

The second prophecy I want to bring to your attention is found in Isaiah 11:

> 10) Then in that day the nations will resort to the root of Jesse, who will stand as a signal for the peoples . . .
>
> 11) Then it will happen on that day that the Lord will again recover the second time with His hand the remnant of His people, who will remain, from Assyria, Egypt, Pathros, Cush, Elam, Shinar, Hamath, and from the islands of the sea.
>
> 12) And He will lift up a standard for the nations and assemble the banished ones of Israel, and will gather the dispersed of Judah from the four corners of the earth.

Some have tried to debunk any modern application of this prophecy by claiming that it was fulfilled about 530 years before the time of Jesus by the return of the Jews from Babylonian captivity. But that cannot be. The passage refers to a "second" regathering (the return from Babylon being the first). Further, it states this will be a regathering "from the islands of the sea," which is a Hebrew colloquialism for the whole world, as is made clear in verse 12 where it states that the regathering will be "from the four corners of the earth." Also, verse 12 says that "the banished ones" of both Israel and Judah will be regathered. The return from Babylon was a regathering of Jews from Judah.

The third prophecy is found in Ezekiel 37. This is the famous prophecy of the Valley of the Dry Bones. The prophet was placed in a valley full of bones and told to preach to them. As he did so, the bones began to come together, flesh grew back upon them and they came to life, becoming "an exceedingly great army" (Ezekiel 37:10). At that point, the Lord explained to Ezekiel what he was witnessing:

> 11) Then He said to me, "Son of man, these bones are the whole house of Israel; behold, they say, 'Our bones are dried up and our hope has perished. We are completely cut off.'
>
> 12) "Therefore prophesy and say to them, 'Thus says the Lord GOD, Behold, I will open your graves and cause you to come up out of your graves, My people; and I will bring you into the land of Israel.'"

This is a symbolic prophecy. The dry bones represent the Jewish people in their end time dispersion, with no hope of ever existing again as a nation. The resurrection from their graves represents their regathering from the nations where they had been dispersed.

We can be assured of this interpretation because it is the one that God Himself provides later in the chapter:

> 21) "Say to them, 'Thus says the Lord GOD, Behold, I will take the sons of Israel from

> among the nations where they have gone, and I will gather them from every side and bring them into their own land;
>
> 22) and I will make them one nation in the land, on the mountains of Israel; and one king will be king for all of them; and they will no longer be two nations and no longer be divided into two kingdoms.'"

Again, those who are determined to argue that God has no purpose left for the Jewish people, attempt to invalidate these verses as an end time prophecy by arguing that they were fulfilled when the Jews returned from Babylonian captivity. But that simply cannot be.

The entire chapter has an end time context. It speaks of a regathering from "the nations," and not just from Babylon (verse 21). It says this regathering will result in a union of Jews from both Israel and Judah (verse 19). And it says that following this regathering, the Jewish people will turn their hearts to God and will become "My people" (verse 23).

At verse 24, the chapter moves into the Millennial Reign of Jesus as it speaks of David (in his glorified body) once again becoming the king of the Jewish people. Further, it states that at that time, "the nations will know that I am the LORD who sanctifies Israel . . ." (verse 28).

The Dreyfus Affair

The fulfillment of these prophecies began in the late 19th Century through the efforts of a Hungarian Jew named Theodor Herzl (1860-1904). He was an intellectual who was serving as a Viennese journalist when the infamous Dreyfus Affair occurred in France.

Alfred Dreyfus (1859-1935) was a young French artillery officer who was Jewish. He was falsely accused of treason in 1894. This accusation occurred in the midst of a wave of anti-

Semitism that had been generated by the publication of a book in 1886 titled, *La France juive* (*Jewish France*).[1] The author, Edouard Drumont (1844-1917), was a virulent anti-Semite who attacked the role of Jews in France and argued for their exclusion from society.[2] The book became wildly popular and went through more than 150 printings before the end of the century.[3]

When the accusation of treason was levied against Dreyfus, the popular press jumped on the band wagon and decided to spotlight the case as proof of Drumont's case against the Jews. They proceeded to whip the general public into a frenzy.

Herzl's Vision

Herzl was sent to Paris to cover the trial for his newspaper. When he arrived, he was shocked by Parisians shouting, "Death to the Jews!"[4] He suddenly experienced an epiphany in which he realized that the Jews had not been assimilated into European society, as he had assumed. Further, he realized they never would be. He sensed an even greater persecution to come.

This realization prompted Herzl to write a brief political booklet called *The Jewish State*, which was published in 1896.[5] In it he called for the return of the Jews to their homeland and the creation of their own state. He argued this would be the best cure to anti-Semitism. His most famous sentence in the book was, "If you will it, it is no dream."

The booklet captured the imagination of Jews all over the world, and it produced the First Zionist Congress, which was held in Basel, Switzerland in 1897. During that conference, Herzl wrote in his diary that he expected the Jewish state to come into existence within 50 years.[6] That statement proved to be prophetic when the United Nations voted 50 years later in 1947 to create a state for the Jewish people.

Another result of Herzl's call for a Jewish homeland was a series of what the Jews called *aliyahs*.[7] These were groups of Jews who decided to pull up stakes in Europe and move back to the land of Palestine, as it was called then, in order to pioneer the land and re-establish a strong Jewish presence.

The Impact of World War I

Another significant development resulted from World War I. The Germans had an ally in that war — namely, the Ottoman Empire of the Turks. This empire controlled all the lands in the Middle East.

When the Germans lost the war, their ally, the Turks, went down with them, and the victorious Allies started dividing up the Ottoman Empire among themselves.

The British were allotted Palestine, which at that time, included both modern day Israel and Jordan. In November 1917, the British issued the Balfour Declaration in which they stated that they "viewed with favor the establishment in Palestine of a national home for the Jewish people . . ."[8]

The Motivation to Return

Still, there was no great surge of Jews who returned to their homeland. The prospect of being a pioneer in the midst of a wilderness was not appealing enough to draw the Jews back home, despite the rising anti-Semitism they were experiencing.

World War I provided the land for the Jewish nation, but it would take World War II and the Holocaust to provide the motivation to return to the land.

The Jewish people came out of the Holocaust proclaiming, "Never again! Never again! We are going to have our own land and our own state, and we are going to govern ourselves!"

In 1900 there were only 40,000 Jews in all of Palestine. By the end of World War II that number had ballooned to over 600,000.[9]

Major Surges of Immigration

The next great surges of immigration resulted from the 1956 Suez War and the 1967 Six Day War. After the Suez War, Egypt expelled almost all of its Jewish population. Following the Six Day War, the rest of the Arab world followed suit.

As a result of these expulsions, almost 800,000 Jews were forcibly expelled from the Arab nations in the Middle East. In 1948 there were 851,000 Jews in the Arab nations of the Middle East. Thirty years later, in 1978, there were only 31,000 left.[10]

But the world's largest Jewish population was unable to return to their homeland because they were held captive in the Soviet Union. The Russians hated the Jews, but they were not willing to let them leave the country because they used them as whipping boys — blaming them for all their nation's problems.

Nonetheless, there was a biblical prophecy that one day the Jews of Russia would be allowed to return to their homeland. It is found in Isaiah 43. The prophet quotes God as saying:

> 4) "Since you are precious in My sight,
> Since you are honored and I love you . . .
>
> 5) "Do not fear, for I am with you;
> I will bring your offspring from the east,
> And gather you from the west.
>
> 6) "I will say to the north, 'Give them up!'
> And to the south, 'Do not hold them back.'
> Bring My sons from afar and My daughters

from the ends of the earth . . ."

Notice that this prophecy says the Jews will come freely from the east and the west, but the world will have to demand that those in the north be released. All directions in the Bible are given from Jerusalem. The uttermost part of the north would be the nation of Russia today. Note also that the prophecy says that the world will have to say to the south, "Do not hold them back." We will see in a moment what that refers to.

But first, let's take a look at the north. In fulfillment of this prophecy, as the Soviet Russian empire began to crumble in the early 1990s, the world began to demand that the Russian Jews be allowed to return to Israel. And in 1990, the Russian premier, Mikhail Gorbachev, suddenly opened the door of the Soviet Union.

The result was a flood of refugees into Israel. During the next two years, almost 400,000 Russian Jews arrived in Israel, averaging over 16,600 a month.[11] It was equivalent to the United States today absorbing the entire 27 million population of Saudi Arabia during the same time period.

Amazingly, the refugees came knowing:

- They would have to abandon all valuables.
- They would face the necessity of learning Hebrew.
- They would have to live in minimal housing.
- They would face military service.
- They would find a non-existent job market.
- They would have to pay some of the highest taxes in the world.
- They would face the constant threat of terrorism and war.

They were fully aware of these stark realities because all of them had relatives living in Israel.

Yet, despite all these hardships, they came. Why? I believe they came, and are still coming, because God has placed in the hearts of the Jewish people the highway to Zion, and He has triggered the impulse for them to return home. Consider Psalm 84:5 — "How blessed is the man whose strength is in You, in whose heart are the highways to Zion!"

Operation Solomon

The largest Jewish population to the south of Jerusalem in the mid-20th Century consisted of the Black Jews of Ethiopia. No one knows for sure the origin of these Jews. The most common speculation is that they resulted from a union between King Solomon and the Queen of Sheba (2 Chronicles 9), but there is no biblical evidence of this. All we know for certain is that they existed in New Testament times because Acts chapter 8 contains the story of an Ethiopian Jew who came to Jerusalem to observe the feasts and who was converted to Christianity on his way back home to Africa by an evangelist named Philip.

In the late 1980s the Jews of Ethiopia began to feel a tug on their hearts to return to the Jewish homeland. In response, they started migrating to Addis Ababa by the thousands where they camped out around the international airport, demanding transportation to Israel. The government adamantly refused to let them leave, in fulfillment of the prophecy in Isaiah 43:6 which states that the Jews in the south will be held back.

But in 1991, as the government began to crumble in the midst of a civil war, the United States and Israel intervened, providing bribes to military leaders. The government then relented and provided a 48 hour window of time for the refugees to depart.

The resulting airlift in May was amazing. In just under 36 hours, 14,500 Ethiopian Jews — nearly the entire Jewish population — was flown to Tel Aviv in 40 flights involving 35 aircraft. At one point there were 28 planes in the air at one time. And a world record was set when one El Al Boeing 747, designed to carry about 350 people, was loaded up with 1,086 passengers. This was possible because all the seats had been stripped out of the plane, the Ethiopians weighed very little, and they had no luggage. When that particular plane reached Tel Aviv, there was a total of 1,088 on board because two babies had been born en route![12]

When I read about that development in the newspapers at the time, I immediately thought of a prophecy in Jeremiah 31:8 which reads as follows: "Behold, I am bringing them from the north country, and I will gather them from the remote parts of the earth, among them the blind and the lame, the woman with child and she who is in labor with child, together; a great company, they will return here."

Today, over 6 million Jews — as many as were killed in the Holocaust — have been gathered back to their homeland, and they are still coming.

The Purpose

Why is God regathering the Jewish people after a dispersion lasting almost 2,000 years?

It's because He has promised that He will bring a remnant of the Jews to salvation before the consummation of history (Zech 12:10, Isaiah 10:20-23 and Romans 9:27). The prophetic scriptures reveal that God has a specific plan for achieving that goal, and we will examine that plan in Part 3 of this book.

The regathering of the Jewish people to their homeland led naturally to the overwhelming desire to re-establish their state. The story of that miraculous event, in fulfillment of prophecy, and the role the United States played in it, is the focus of chapter 6.

Chapter 6

The Re-establishment of the State of Israel

In 2008 Israel celebrated its 60th anniversary as an independent state. The celebration was held on May 8th (the 5th of Iyar on the Jewish calendar).

In 1948 the 5th of Iyar fell on May 14th, and that was the momentous day when David Ben Gurion read the Israeli Declaration of Independence at a small museum in Tel Aviv before an audience of about 200 people. Only one photographer was present.

The first nation to recognize the new state was the United States. President Harry S. Truman issued the recognition statement only 11 minutes after the declaration went into effect. American recognition proved to be one of the crucial keys to the survival of Israel. What prompted President Truman to act so quickly and so decisively? It's only in recent years that the full story has emerged.

The International Setting

But first, some background. In the last chapter I talked about the importance of the Balfour Declaration which the British issued in November 1917. The Jewish leaders interpreted it to mean that the Jewish people could return to their ancient homeland and ultimately re-establish their state.

Again, at that time, Palestine consisted of all of modern day Israel and Jordan — an area of 45,000 square miles.

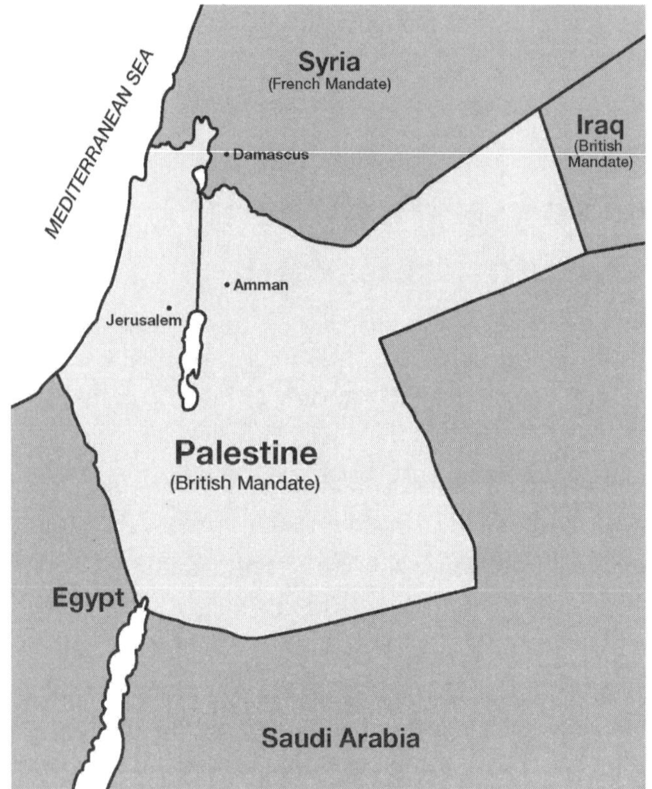

Palestine in 1917

But hardly had the ink dried on the Balfour Declaration before the British decided in 1922 to give two-thirds of Palestine to the Arabs in order to secure their access to Arab oil. This led to the creation of a Palestinian state called Transjordan (see the map on the next page).

This British action to placate the Arabs left a small area of land for the promised Jewish state — a sliver of land only 10,000 square miles in size, smaller than Lake Michigan or the state of New Jersey.

The League of Nations Mandate

Immediately thereafter, the League of Nations entrusted what was left of Palestine to Britain as a Mandate, and the

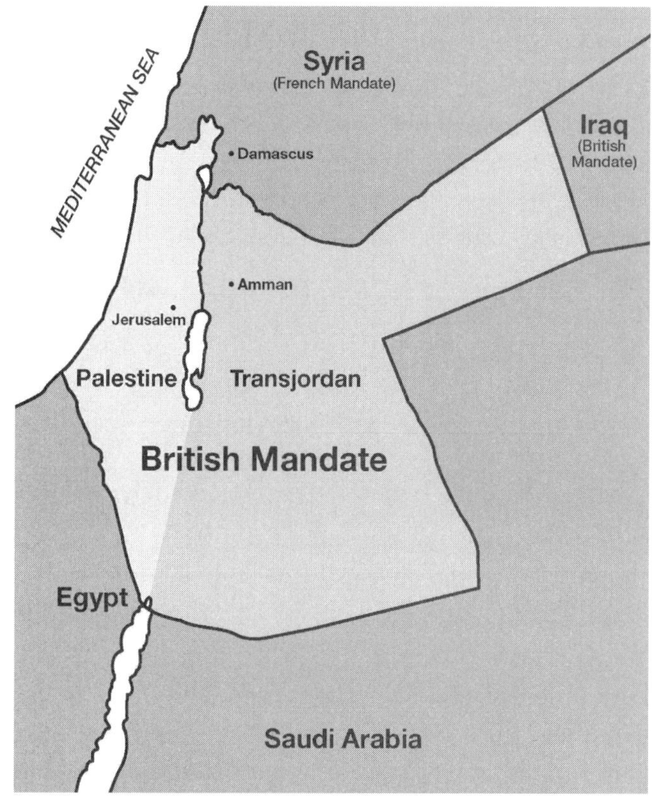

British Division of Palestine in 1922

British began to rule the land with the ultimate goal of guiding it to self-government. But the British soon found themselves in the middle of a bloody Jewish-Arab struggle for the land.

As the struggle intensified and more and more British soldiers were killed, the British people began to pressure the government to look for a way to extricate themselves from the bloodbath. The pressure mounted in late 1946 when Winston Churchill, leader of the opposition to the Labor Government, began publicly urging an end to the Mandate. He declared, "If we cannot fulfill our promises to the Zionists, we should, without delay, place our Mandate for Palestine at the feet of the United Nations, and give them due notice of our impending evacuation from the country."[1]

At about the same time, in October 1946, President Truman endorsed the establishment of a "viable Jewish state" in Palestine.[2] Most people assumed that the timing of this announcement was probably prompted by the mid-term elections for Congress that were coming up in November.

Delivering the Problem to the United Nations

Clement Attlee (British Prime Minister from 1945 to 1951) reluctantly gave ground to the mounting pressure. On February 18, 1947, Attlee's spokesman announced: "His Majesty's Government have of themselves no power under the terms of the Mandate to award the country to the Arabs or the Jews, or even to partition it between them . . . We have, therefore, reached the conclusion that the only course open to us is to submit the problem to the judgment of the United Nations."[3]

This action by the British government was most likely a ruse to satisfy public opinion, for no one in the government believed that there were enough votes in the United Nations to end the Mandate. The Russians and their allies were staunchly pro-Arab, and their bloc, together with the Arab states, represented enough votes to prevent a British withdrawal that might lead to a partition of the land which the Arabs wanted all to themselves.

The British announcement led to the calling of a special session of the General Assembly of the United Nations to deal with what was dubbed as "The Palestine Question." The session was held at Flushing Meadows, New York, from April 28th to May 15th of 1947.

Two significant developments came out of this special session. First, the General Assembly decided to set up an eleven member investigating committee called The United Nations Special Committee on Palestine (UNSCOP). Its purpose was to study the problem of Palestine and propose a solution.[4]

The second development was a diplomatic bombshell in the form of a surprise announcement by the Soviet Ambassador, Andrei Gromyko. He attacked what he called the "bankruptcy of the mandatory system of Palestine" and then went on to endorse "the aspirations of the Jews to establish their own state."[5]

Why the Russians did this about-face is still a mystery to this day. Most likely, they were motivated by a desire to force the British to withdraw from the Middle East, believing that the much more numerous Arabs could fill the resulting political vacuum, ending up with a weak Arab state that would be dependent on the Soviets. Whatever the reason, the Russian move caught the British flat-footed. They were suddenly faced with the reality that the process had gone too far for them to put the brakes on it.

The United Nations Solution

In late August of 1947 the UNSCOP report was released. The Committee agreed unanimously to recommend ending the Mandate as soon as possible. The majority (7 to 3, with one abstention) recommended partition of Palestine into Arab and Jewish states. The minority called for a federation with Arab and Jewish cantons.[6] The Jews reluctantly accepted the report. The Arabs passionately rejected it and threatened war should the United Nations approve partition.

The UNSCOP proposal produced an Arab state composed of three areas: the Gaza Strip, the Central Highlands of Judea and Samaria, and the Western Galilee (see the map on the next page).

These areas were intertwined serpent-like with the areas allotted to Israel: the Eastern Galilee, the Coastal Plain, and the Negev Desert. The Arab state would embrace 4,500

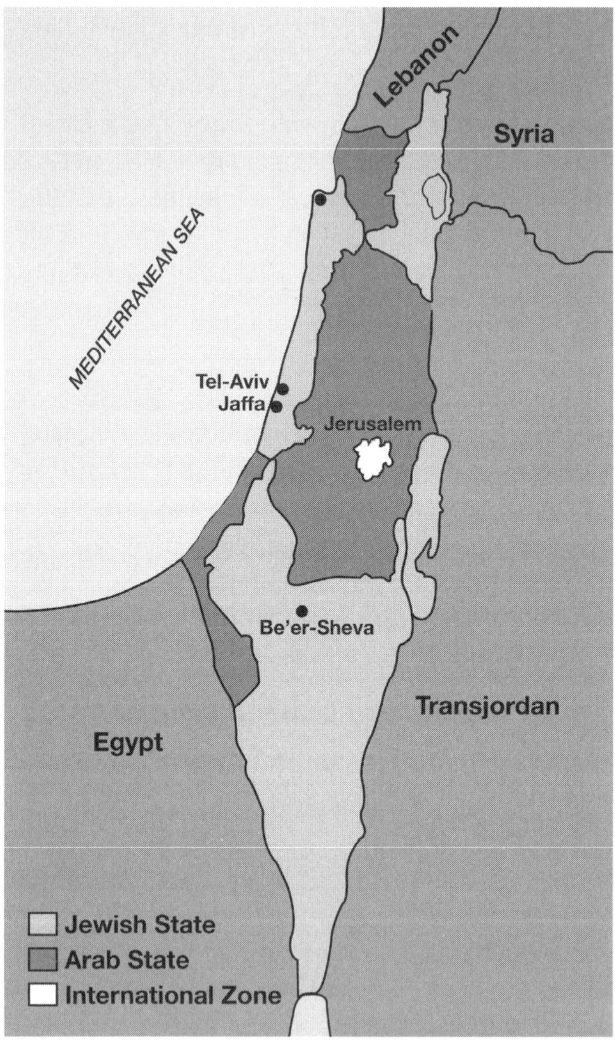

UN Partition Plan - 1947

square miles, with 840,000 Arabs and 10,000 Jews. The Jewish state would encompass 5,500 square miles, with 538,000 Jews and 397,000 Arabs. Jerusalem and Bethlehem were to be internationalized. These cities contained a combined total of 100,000 Jews and the same number of Arabs.[7]

On November 29, 1947, the United Nations voted to adopt the UNSCOP recommendations to partition Palestine and create both Jewish and Arab states. The vote in favor totaled 33 and included the United States and Russia. Thirteen voted against, including all eleven Muslim states. There were ten abstentions, including Britain. The resolution required a two-thirds vote of those voting, so it passed with votes to spare. The deciding bloc turned out to be the nations of Latin America. All of them, with the exception of Cuba, voted in favor of the resolution.[8]

Jews all over the world broke out in rejoicing, but the Jewish leaders knew that the fight was not over. As the Arabs rattled their sabers, the Jews launched a massive public relations campaign aimed at keeping the United States committed to partition.

The Response to the United Nations Vote

In December of 1947 the White House received more than 100,000 letters and telegrams concerning Palestine.[9] In the midst of the escalating and conflicting pressure, President Truman wrote to one of his assistants: "I surely wish God Almighty would give the Children of Israel an Isaiah, the Christians a St. Paul, and the Sons of Ishmael a peep at the Golden Rule."[10]

On December 3rd the British announced they would terminate their League of Nations Mandate for Palestine on May 15, 1948. That same day the Arabs announced they would "defend their rights."[11]

The British announcement and the hostile Arab response to it prompted a reconsideration of the American position in support of partition. The speed at which the process was moving seemed to spook the State and Defense Departments.

James Forrestal, the Secretary of Defense, together with the Joint Chiefs of Staff, reminded President Truman of the critical need for Saudi Arabian oil. The President responded by saying he would "handle the situation in light of justice, not oil."[12] Forrestal also told the President that in his opinion, "the Arabs would push the Jews into the sea."[13]

The pressure from the State Department was even more intense because its career bureaucrats were all pro-Arab. They began to develop an alternative to the partition plan. Their idea was to replace the League of Nations Mandate with a United Nations Trusteeship.[14] As the new year of 1948 arrived, extreme tension mounted between the White House and what President Truman called "the striped pants boys" at the State Department.[15]

The President's contempt for the State Department did not apply to his Secretary of State, General George C. Marshall, even though Marshall was the strongest opponent to the establishment of the Jewish state. Truman greatly admired Marshall, and Marshall had the highest degree of public respect of anyone in the Truman Administration. The Secretary's "Marshall Plan" for the reconstruction of Europe had caught the public imagination and had been hailed as a lifesaver throughout Europe. Marshall's outstanding leadership resulted in his being selected as *Time* magazine's "Man of the Year" for 1947. Regarding Palestine, Marshall favored a "unitary state under a United Nations Trusteeship."[16]

There were only two people in the Truman Administration who strongly supported the partition plan, and both of them were presidential advisers — David Niles and Clark Clifford. Clifford was Truman's White House Counsel and confidant. Niles, who was Jewish, was one of only two Roosevelt aides who were retained by Truman when he became President. Niles was the President's counselor regarding minority issues and patronage.

As a Jew, Niles had a natural sympathy for the terrible plight of the Jewish people who had survived the Holocaust.

Clifford, on the other hand, based his support of Israel on his reading of ancient history and the Bible. He firmly believed the Jewish people were entitled to their homeland.[17] Niles kept the key Zionist leaders informed of what was going on in Washington and within the White House. Clifford served to encourage the President to hold firm to his commitment to a Jewish state.

When the Zionist leaders learned of the strong opposition within the Truman Administration to the establishment of a Jewish state, they decided to send their foremost statesman and spokesman to Washington, D.C., to confer with the President. He was Chaim Weizmann (1874-1952).[18]

Two Crucial Jewish Voices

Dr. Weizmann was a Russian Jew who had migrated to England where he had become a professor of chemistry. During World War I he greatly aided the British when he developed a synthetic form of acetone which was essential in the manufacture of cordite explosive. Some historians have suggested that this contribution to the British war effort is what prompted the Balfour Declaration. Weizmann served twice as president of the World Zionist Organization (1921-1931 and 1935-1946).

Despite his immense prestige, when Weizmann arrived in Washington, D.C., in March 1948, President Truman refused to see him. This was because the President had become irritated over all the Jewish pressure that was being applied to the White House, particularly by some American rabbis who had been very tactless. Also, the President had already met with Dr. Weizmann the previous November, and during that meeting, the President had assured him of his support for a Jewish state.[19]

It was at this critical point in time that President Truman's dear friend and former business partner, Eddie Jacobson, decided to intervene. The two had been partners in the clothing store business in Kansas City from 1919 to 1922. In his memoirs, Truman wrote that he never had a "truer friend."[20]

Jacobson was Jewish. He was not a Zionist, but he had a great compassion for the sufferings of the Jewish people. When he learned that Truman was refusing to see Weizmann, he traveled to Washington, D.C., to urge his old business partner to change his mind. Truman was impressed: "In all my years in Washington," he wrote, "he had never asked me for anything for himself."[21]

In response to Jacobson's fervent personal plea, President Truman agreed to see Dr. Weizmann off-the-record on March 18th. They talked for almost an hour, and once again, the President assured Weizmann of his support for a Jewish state.[22]

A Diplomatic Earthquake

The very next day the State Department blind-sided the President when Warren Austin, the U.S. Ambassador to the United Nations, announced that the United States had decided to recommend abandoning the partition plan in favor of a UN Trusteeship![23] Truman wrote with a fury in his diary:[24]

> This morning I find that the State Department has reversed my Palestine policy. The first I know about it is what I see in the papers. Isn't that hell? I'm now in the position of a liar and a double-crosser. I never felt so [before] in my life.

Truman was particularly infuriated because he had specifically insisted that he be shown Austin's speech in advance. The State Department had ignored this command.[25] What made the situation even more painful was that the President could not publicly repudiate Austin. To do so would make it appear that he was not in control of his own foreign policy. Reflecting upon this event in his memoirs, Truman wrote:[26]

> The difficulty with many career officials in the government is that they regard themselves as the men who really make policy and run the government. They look upon elected officials as just temporary occupants. Every President in our history has been faced with this problem: how to prevent career men from circumventing presidential policy.

Eddie Jacobson returned to the White House on April 11th to urge the President to reverse the State Department announcement. The President assured him "very strongly" that he supported partition and was determined to recognize the new Jewish state.[27]

The Final Show-Down

But the opponents of partition within the Administration were determined to change the President's mind. Their all-out effort occurred on May 12th when Secretary of State Marshall and several of his aides went to the White House to meet with the President. To their surprise, President Truman had several of his aides present, including David Niles and Clark Clifford.

The meeting began with a presentation by one of Secretary Marshall's aides, Robert Lovett. He presented the State Department's case for a United Nations Trusteeship.

The President then called on Clark Clifford to read a paper he had prepared. In that paper Clifford argued that the recognition of the state of Israel would be "an act of humanity" in response to the Holocaust. He quoted the promise of the Balfour Declaration and he cited verses from Deuteronomy to verify the Jewish claim to the land.[28]

Marshall became incensed. He considered Clifford to be nothing more than a political operative, and he believed his arguments were politically motivated, designed to guarantee the Jewish vote for the President in the upcoming election. Marshall finally became so agitated that he interrupted Clifford and said, "This is just straight politics. I don't even understand why Clifford is here!" Truman answered softly, "General, he is here because I asked him to be here."

Clifford continued. When he finished, Lovett spoke again in rebuttal. He argued that recognition of the Jewish state would be disastrous to American prestige at the United Nations because it would appear only as "a transparent bid" for Jewish votes in the upcoming presidential election in November.

At this point, Marshall spoke again. Looking directly at Truman, he said that if the President were to follow Clifford's advice, he would vote against the President in the election!

It was an incredible rebuke of the President in front of witnesses. The room fell silent. All sat in shock. Clifford later called it an "awful, total silence." Truman showed no sign of emotion. Finally, he said he thought it would be best for everyone to "sleep on the matter."[29]

The Final Decision

Two days later, on Friday, May 14th, the day of the Declaration of Independence, Secretary of State Marshall called the President and told him that while he could not personally support recognition, he would not oppose it publicly.[30]

The Declaration was scheduled to take effect at 6:00 pm Washington time. Eleven minutes after the effective time, one of the President's aides, Charlie Ross, announced that the United States was granting *de facto* recognition to the new state of Israel. The United States thus became the very first nation to recognize Israel.

The American delegation to the United Nations was flabbergasted. Marshall dispatched his head of UN affairs,

Dean Acheson, by plane to New York to keep the whole delegation from resigning. Many in the State Department urged Marshall to resign, but he refused. He said the President had the constitutional right to make the decision. However, he refused ever again to speak to Clark Clifford.[31]

The Aftermath

On May 15, the British High Commissioner in Palestine said his farewells and departed Jerusalem. The following day the Provisional Government of Israel met and elected Dr. Chaim Weizmann to serve as Israel's first president.

Meanwhile the fledgling Jewish state had come under immediate attack from five Arab armies who were determined to destroy the nation at its birth. Attacking from three sides, the armies came from Egypt, Transjordan, Iraq, Syria, and Lebanon.

This invasion fulfilled a symbolic prophecy given by Isaiah in which he said that the future Jewish state would be born "in one day" and that the labor pains would come *after* the birth (Isaiah 66:7-8). And so they did, and those labor pains have continued to this day as Israel has experienced one war after another for its survival.

After Truman's re-election in November 1948, the Chief Rabbi of Israel, Isaac HaLevi Herzog, paid the President a visit. He told Truman, "I believe God put you in your mother's womb so you would be the instrument to bring the rebirth of Israel after two thousand years."[32]

In May 1951, David Ben Gurion, the Prime Minister of Israel, visited the President at the White House to thank him for his support. His last meeting with the President occurred in 1952 at a hotel in New York. In an interview which he gave years later, he said:[33]

> I told him [Truman] that as a foreigner I could not judge what would be his place in

> American history; but his helpfulness to us, his constant sympathy with our aims in Israel, his courageous decision to recognize our new state so quickly, and his steadfast support since then had given him an immortal place in Jewish history. As I said that, tears suddenly sprang to his eyes. And his eyes were still wet when he bade me goodbye . . . A little later . . . a correspondent came up to me and asked, "Why was President Truman in tears when he left you?"

Motivations

Was Secretary of State Marshall correct in his assessment of President Truman's motivations? Was the President's decision concerning Palestine motivated by politics?

On the surface, this would be easy to believe. After all, New York state had more Jews than the state of Israel, and the President was facing what seemed to be impossible odds. His popularity rating was low and his party was split three ways. Senator Strom Thurmond of South Carolina was pulling out to run as the candidate of the Dixiecrat Party, a move that threatened to take the Southern states away from the President. And FDR's former Secretary of Agriculture and Vice President, Henry Wallace, was determined to run on the Progressive Party ticket. This move threatened to attract the liberal wing of the Democrats.

But despite these political matters, the historical record seems to indicate that Truman's decision was deeply rooted in his personal values and his Christian faith. All his life he was a voracious reader. He always claimed that he had read the Bible twice before he even started to school! He knew the history of the Jews by heart, and he understood their biblical claim to the land.[34]

His heart was revealed early on in April of 1943 when he was serving in the Congress as a Senator from Missouri. He flew to Chicago to speak at a huge rally that was held at Chicago Stadium to urge help for the doomed Jews of Europe. There was no political gain to be made from such an appearance, but Truman went anyway, and he spoke with great passion.

He referred to Hitler as a "madman," and he boldly implied criticism of President Roosevelt for not doing enough to help the Jews. Referring to FDR's "Four Freedoms" speech, Truman observed:[35]

> Merely talking about the Four Freedoms is not enough. This is the time for action. No one can any longer doubt the horrible intentions of the Nazi beasts. We know they plan the systematic slaughter throughout all of Europe, not only of the Jews, but of vast numbers of other innocent peoples.

Proverbs 21:1 states that the hearts of rulers are like "channels of water in the hand of the Lord." The passage goes on to state that God can turn their hearts "wherever He wishes."

The story of Harry Truman's decision to support the establishment of a Jewish state and grant it immediate recognition is a story about how God prepares a man to make an historic decision that would fulfill Bible prophecy.

First, Truman was grounded in the Scriptures and was well-acquainted with the history of the Jews. Then, a Jewish man he met in the military during World War I became his best friend and business partner. He was deeply impacted by the suffering of the Jewish people during the Holocaust. And when the time came for his momentous decision regarding Palestine, two of his closest advisors were staunch supporters of Israel. The Lord even touched the heart of Israel's greatest opponent within the Administration — Secretary of State George Marshall — and at the very last moment, he consented to the President's course of action.

How else can the pivotal role of Eddie Jacobson be explained, except supernaturally? He was a simple store clerk whom God positioned in the center of Truman's life, ready to take action at just the right moment.

The Bible says that God made a promise to Abraham that He would bless those who bless the Jews and curse those who curse them (Genesis 12:3). God has been faithful to that promise throughout history.

In May of 1948, President Harry S. Truman greatly blessed the Jewish people. In November, God returned the blessing to him as he won re-election in one of the most astounding victories in American history.

Prophecies Concerning the Rebirth of the State

The re-establishment of the State of Israel is the cornerstone even of end time Bible prophecy — the clearest indicator that we are in the season of the Messiah's return.

The prophet Zechariah clearly foresaw this day when he spoke of a time when the Jews would be regathered and would reoccupy Jerusalem (Zechariah 8). He said that at that time their nation would be empowered by the Lord to the point that it would be like David against Goliath as it dealt with its enemies (Zechariah 12:6-8).

Ezekiel also prophesied about the state of Israel in the end times. He said the Jewish people would be regathered and re-established in the land at which time they would be "an exceedingly great army" (Ezekiel 37:1-10). He even prophesied that the revived state would be called Israel, as opposed to Zion or Judah, as some of the Jewish leaders desired (Ezekiel 37:12).

But my favorite prophecy about the re-establishment of the state is a symbolic one found in Isaiah 66:7-8 which reads as follows:

> 7) "Before she travailed, she brought forth; before her pain came, she gave birth to a boy.
>
> 8) "Who has heard such a thing? Who has seen such things? Can a land be born in one day? Can a nation be brought forth all at once?"

What an incredible prophecy! It says the state will be born in one day and that the birth pains will follow! And that is exactly what happened. The state was declared on May 14, 1948, and the next day the birth pains began as five Arab nations invaded the fledgling new state. And those birth pains have continued to this day.

Chapter 7

The Revival of the Hebrew Language

For many years I have been taking pilgrimage groups to the Holy Land. One of the places we always visit is the Dead Sea Scrolls Museum in Jerusalem. The centerpiece of the museum is the Isaiah scroll that is displayed in a circular glass case.

I usually gather my group around the scroll, explain its importance and then turn the group loose to explore the rest of the museum. One year, after releasing the group, as I was walking away from the Isaiah scroll, I heard someone behind me suddenly start speaking loudly in Hebrew. When I turned around to see who it was, I discovered a young boy about 13 years old with his parents. The boy was reading the scroll, using a pointer. I supposed he was practicing for his Bar Mitzvah, for reading a section from the Scriptures is always a part of that ceremony.

As I listened to the young man, I realized I was witnessing a miracle. It occurred to me that a Greek boy of his age could not read the Greek writings of Homer (ca. 8th Century BC) nor could an American or British boy read the English of Chaucer (14th Century AD). Yet this boy could read Hebrew written 2,000 years ago!

How was that possible? Because biblical Hebrew has been revived from the dead and is spoken as the national language of Israel today.

The Death of the Hebrew Language

But I am getting ahead of my story. Let's return for a moment to the days of the Bible.

As the Jewish people were scattered worldwide, they gradually stopped speaking their native language during the centuries that followed. Those in Europe took German and mixed it with Hebrew, producing a hybrid tongue called Yiddish. The Jews who settled in the Mediterranean basin mixed Hebrew with Spanish and developed a language called Ladino.

Hebrew became confined to the synagogues where it was used for Torah readings. By the beginning of the 20th Century, most Jews could not understand the Torah readings. For them, it was like a Gentile experiencing a Catholic mass conducted in Latin.

But all this was to change miraculously, and in the process, the fulfillment of a very important end time Bible prophecy began.

The Key Prophecy

The prophecy I have in mind is one about the revival of the Hebrew language. It is found in Zephaniah 3:9 —

> For then I will restore to the peoples a pure language, that they all may call on the name of the LORD, to serve Him with one accord. (*New King James Version*)

The *New International Version* states that the Lord will "purify the lips of the people." The *New Living Translation* says God will "purify the speech." The *English Standard Version* puts it this way: "I will change the speech of the peoples to a pure speech." *The Living Bible* paraphrases the verse to read: "At that time I will change the speech of my returning people to pure Hebrew so that all can worship the Lord together."

The more literal translations of this verse leave the clear implication that the ultimate fulfillment of this prophecy will occur when all the peoples of the world are once again unified in their language, likely speaking biblical Hebrew. Whether this will occur during the Millennium or the Eternal State is not made precisely clear in the Scriptures.

For example, Isaiah 19:18 says that during the Lord's millennial reign, there will be cities in Egypt where people will be speaking Hebrew. And our key verse, Zephaniah 3:9, is set in the context of being fulfilled after God has poured out His "indignation" on the nations (Zephaniah 3:8). That's speaking of the Tribulation, so the implication is that the establishment of a universal language will occur at the beginning of the Millennium.

On the other hand, Zechariah 8:23 tells us that during the Millennium, "ten people from all languages and nations will take hold of one Jew by the hem of his robe and say, 'Let us go with you, because we have heard that God is with you'" (NIV). So, it sounds like national languages will continue during the Millennium, and thus the unity of language will not occur until we reach the Eternal State.

But, as you will see, the revival of biblical Hebrew as the spoken language of the Jewish people today must be considered a miracle of God and at least a partial fulfillment of Zephaniah 3:9. In that regard, it should be noted that there is no other example in world history of an ancient language being revived as the spoken language of a modern nation. The restoration of biblical Hebrew to a modern day spoken language is a unique historical phenomenon.

The Key Person

God orchestrated the revival of spoken Hebrew through a baby born to an Orthodox Jewish family in 1858 in Lithuania, which at that time was part of Russia. He was given the name of Eliezer Yitzhak Perlman.

When Eliezer was 5 years old, his father died of tuberculosis. A few years later, the boy was sent to live with his mother's wealthy uncle, who was a stern taskmaster. As soon as Eliezer turned 13 and celebrated his Bar Mitzvah, he was sent to a yeshiva (Rabbinical training school) in Belarus. There he fell under the influence of a young progressive rabbi who was caught up in the Jewish Enlightenment Movement.

The Key Teacher

One day the rabbi asked Eliezer to stay after class. When all the other students had left, the rabbi handed Eliezer a book and asked him to read it aloud. It was a Hebrew translation of *Robinson Crusoe*, and Eliezer was amazed by it.[1] This was in 1872.

Eliezer's amazement was rooted in the fact that Orthodox Jews considered the Hebrew language to be a holy language that was appropriate only for use in the synagogue and for Rabbinical writing.[2] To use it for secular purposes was considered ungodly and blasphemous.[3] In fact it was taken to be an attack on the Jewish religion.[4]

From the moment Eliezer saw that Hebrew could be used for other than liturgical purposes, he was hooked on it and its revival as a spoken language. Near the end of his life, while thinking back on that moment, he wrote: "Since the first glance at a Hebrew *Robinson Crusoe*, I fell in love with the Hebrew tongue as a living language. This love was a great and all-consuming fire that the torrent of life could not extinguish."[5]

The Key Situation

Eliezer had grown up with Yiddish as his natural spoken language. He was a prodigy, so at the age of three he was reading Hebrew in the Scriptures and prayer books. But it was not used for everyday conversation, and not only because it was considered holy. Another problem was the fact that it did not contain sufficient words to carry on a modern day conversation.

It is estimated that in the 1880s only about 50 percent of all male Jews could understand the Hebrew readings in the synagogue, and as few as 20 percent could read a book written in Hebrew.[6] In that same decade, the Jewish poet, Yehuda Leib Gordon (1830-1892) wrote: "Perhaps I am the last of Zion's poets, and you are the last readers."[7] Although Gordon was a part of the Jewish Enlightenment, he saw little hope for Hebrew becoming a daily spoken language or even a language of literature.

Hebrew, because of its lack of use, was just too clumsy. One of Eliezer's biographers summed it up this way:[8]

> Young writers preferred to write in Yiddish or in a European language, full of feeling and color. By contrast, Hebrew was bare and stiff, the dry language of the scholar. No one used Hebrew for everyday expressions. Orthodox Jews had a different reason for not speaking Hebrew. They believed it was wrong to use a holy language to say something like, "Take out the garbage."

Moshe Lilienblum (1843-1910), who was considered the "dean" of Hebrew authors at the time Eliezer was introduced to *Robinson Crusoe* in Hebrew, was also disillusioned with the future of the language. In a newspaper article, he announced that "Hebrew's time has passed, and it no longer has a purpose or task in Jewish life."[9]

The Key Family

When Eliezer's great-uncle discovered that the boy had fallen under the influence of a teacher mixed-up in the Jewish Enlightenment, he pulled him out of the yeshiva and disowned him. Eliezer wandered about on his own and ended up at a synagogue in Russia. There he met a remarkable man named Solomon Jonas who asked the boy to come live with his family. Jonas was a wealthy whiskey maker with six children of his own, the oldest of which was a daughter named Deborah who was 18 years old.[10]

Eliezer lived with this family for the next two years and was tutored by Deborah in French, German and Russian. During that time, his heart grew fond of Deborah.[11]

When Eliezer was 16, his adopted father decided he needed to pursue his education at a state school in Latvia. But this, as we will see, was not the end of Eliezer's relationship with the Jonas family.

It is significant to note that during his stay with the Jonas family, Eliezer developed a constant cough.[12]

The Key Event

Eliezer's time at the state school was to prove to be a pivotal period in his life. During that time he was introduced to the concept of nationalism, and he became a zealot in behalf of it.

In 1877 Russia went to war against the Ottoman Empire in behalf of the liberation of the Balkans. And the concept of nationalism — "one state for each nation" — became the battle cry that swept Europe and which ultimately led to the outbreak of World War I.

The war in the Balkans captured Eliezer's imagination and awakened within him the idea that the Jewish nation, like all other nations, deserved its own state. Here's how he explained it:[13]

> After a number of hours of reading the papers and reflecting on the fate of the Bulgarians and their future freedom, suddenly, as if lightning struck, an incandescent light radiated before my eyes . . . and I heard a strange inner

> voice calling to me: "The revival of Israel and its language in the land of the forefathers!". . The lot was cast. My life and strength were given from that time on to the labor of reviving Israel and its tongue in the land of the fathers.

The Key Diagnosis

In 1878, at the age of 20, Eliezer arrived in Paris where he intended to study medicine. But his heart was in Palestine, as his homeland was called at that time. And his zeal was for the revival of the Hebrew language as a spoken tongue.

But all his dreams and hopes were suddenly derailed by his nagging cough. He finally went to a doctor for a diagnosis, and the news he received was devastating. He had developed tuberculosis.

He immediately wrote to Deborah to inform her. "I have the feeling of a person condemned to death," he wrote. He continued, "For this reason I work now without sleep to put onto paper the reasons why it is so important for the Jewish world to become inflamed with the idea of returning to the land of our forefathers . . ."[14] He then focused in on his greatest concern:[15]

> I have decided that in order to have our own land and political life, it is also necessary that we have a language to hold us together. That language is Hebrew, but not the Hebrew of the rabbis and scholars. We must have a Hebrew language in which we can conduct the business of life. It will not be easy to revive a language dead for so long a time.

Eliezer closed this letter with a statement that would become his lifelong motto: "The day is short; the work to be done is so great!"

In his next letter to Deborah, he signed it Ben-Yehuda, and he added this postscript: "Do not be surprised that I sign a new name to my letter. This is the name which will appear over my articles. Someday I shall find the way to make it my own."[16]

His new name had a double meaning. His father's given name had been Leib, which was Yiddish for Yehuda. Thus, Ben-Yehuda meant Son of Yehuda. But Yehuda is the Hebrew word for Judea, and so the new name also meant that he considered himself to be a Son of Judea — a son of the land of his forefathers.[17]

The Key Articles

In 1879, when Ben-Yehuda was only 21, a prestigious Vienna newspaper published an article of his titled, "A Burning Question." The editor changed the name to "A Weighty Question." It was to be one of the first ever Zionist manifestos, calling on the Jewish people to return to their homeland.

In the article, Ben-Yehuda became the first person to call for the revival of Hebrew as an everyday language.[18] In the process of writing the essay, Ben-Yehuda had to invent a new Hebrew word for nationalism: *leumiut*.[19] He signed the article with his new name — Eliezer Ben-Yehuda.

Predictably, the Orthodox Jews reacted furiously, denouncing Ben-Yehuda as a pagan because he had the audacity to suggest that their holy language be defiled by using it for everyday conversation.[20] But Ben-Yehuda was not deterred. He immediately responded to his critics with a second article which he titled, "And We Have Still Not Learned Our Lesson."[21]

In it he decried the political and philosophical divisions among the Jewish people and called for unity. He wrote, "Why do we not see, all of us whose eyes are so keen, that if we do not hurry to unite, the end is near, the horrible end of the hope of our people for an eventual redemption?" He then proceeded to ask a rhetorical question: "What is this one point on which all of us can unite?" His obvious answer: "The resettlement of the Land of Israel."[22]

A Key Discovery

In 1880 Ben-Yehuda decided to take the advice of his doctor and go to Algiers in North Africa where he was assured the climate would be much better for his health. The advice proved true.

But what turned out to be more significant was a linguistic discovery Ben-Yehuda made there. For the first time, he encountered Hebrew as spoken by Sephardic Jews — the Jews who had settled around the rim of the Mediterranean Sea. He discovered that their pronunciation of Hebrew was so different from his Ashkenazic pronunciation that he could not understand them, nor could they understand him.[23]

As he studied their system of pronunciation, he fell in love with it. He found it to be more flowing and melodic, more natural to the lips and easier on the ears.[24] Deciding rather arbitrarily, Ben-Yehuda concluded that the Sephardic pronunciation had to be closer to the original in biblical times, and he demanded it and taught it from that day forward.[25]

The Key Land

Although the climate of North Africa was very beneficial to Ben-Yehuda's health, he decided that if he was destined to die from TB, he would die in his homeland. So he decided to move to Palestine and reside in Jerusalem.

This was an incredible decision for anyone in that day and time, especially for a sick person. Palestine was a barren wasteland full of great hardships, and Jerusalem was an incubator of diseases — a backwater town where the sewage ran down the middle of the streets.

Before departing, Ben-Yehuda felt compelled to write Solomon Jonas and let him know he had decided not to marry Deborah because any wife of his would face terrible hardships and diseases and the possibility that he might die at any moment.[26] But despite this letter and the fact they had not seen each other in seven years, Deborah would have none of it. She wrote back and insisted they get married. She stated that she was as bound to his fate as Ruth of biblical times had been bound to the fate of her mother-in-law, Naomi.[27]

They were married in Cairo in 1881. She was 27; he was 23. They agreed that Deborah's name would be changed to the Hebrew equivalent of D'vorah.[28] They also agreed that they would never again speak to each other in any language except Hebrew — despite the fact that D'vorah spoke little Hebrew and the language lacked words for many everyday things.[29] This led to communication through a lot of hand signals and finger pointing over the next few years.[30]

The couple proceeded immediately to Palestine and arrived at the port of Jaffa in the fall of 1881. From there they traveled by carriage to Jerusalem where Ben-Yehuda resided for the next 41 years. Many years later, Ben-Yehuda wrote that he had only two regrets in life: "There are two things for which I am sorry, and for which I can find no consolation: I was not born in Jerusalem, or even in the Land of Israel, and the first words I spoke were not spoken in Hebrew."[31]

The Key City

For 2,000 years, ever since their expulsion from the land by the Romans, the Jews in the Diaspora had been ending their Passover meals with the prayer, "Next year in Jerusalem." At long last that prayer had been answered for Eliezer and D'vorah. But the Jerusalem they found was not the Jerusalem of Scripture which is referred to in Isaiah as "a crown of beauty in the hand of the Lord" (62:3) and "a praise in the earth" (62:7).

Instead, the city proved to be what they had been warned it would be. They found a small town of only 25,000 residents who were living in filth.[32] The Jews constituted about half the population, but they were divided up into close-knit communities that had little to do with each other. And to Ben-Yehuda's despair, he discovered them speaking Ladino, Yiddish, Arabic, Spanish and Russian — but no Hebrew.[33]

At first, they tried to court the Orthodox community by dressing like Sephardic Jews, observing the kosher laws and attending the synagogue services on the Sabbath.[34] But this effort proved to be of no avail. Ben-Yehuda's reputation as a Zionist with the aim of reviving Hebrew as a spoken language had preceded him. The result was that the Orthodox community, especially the Ashkenazis (European Jews), ostracized them.

Ultimately, this treatment convinced Ben-Yehuda and his wife that they should return to European ways and dress. Accordingly, Ben-Yehuda cut off his side curls, shaved his long beard into a close-cut goatee and started wearing suits instead of robes.[35] This change convinced the Orthodox that they had been right all along in viewing the couple as pagans.

Ben-Yehuda's zeal became focused. He made a large sign of his motto ("The day is short; the work to be done is so great!"), and he hung it on the wall above his stand-up desk (he argued that he could think better standing up).[36] He proceeded to work 15 to 19 hours each day, most of it standing!

The Key Plan

Ben-Yehuda had a very specific plan in mind when he arrived in Jerusalem, and he pursued it fanatically and methodically. It consisted of several elements:[37]

- Encourage the speaking of Hebrew in each home.
- Establish a newspaper and work through it to report the news in Hebrew, creating new words as needed.
- Do everything possible to introduce the teaching and speaking of Hebrew into the schools.
- Produce a dictionary of the Hebrew language to aid in its daily utilization.

Hebrew in the Home

Ben-Yehuda began the implementation of his plan by starting with his own home. He laid down the rule that no language could be spoken within his house except Hebrew. He wanted his family to be a model for others. And thus, when D'vorah became pregnant, he announced that the baby she was carrying would become the first true Hebrew child in 2,000 years because it would be allowed to hear only biblical Hebrew.[38] That meant no playmates, and it meant almost total isolation at home.

Their friends were aghast over such fanaticism. They pleaded with Ben-Yehuda to change his mind, arguing that the child would grow up either as a mute or an idiot.[39] But Ben-Yehuda would not budge.

In 1882 D'vorah gave birth to this first child, a boy who was named Ben-Zion Ben-Yehuda, meaning Son of Zion and Son of Judea.[40] And just as Ben-Yehuda had promised, the son was kept isolated from the world so that he would not become "contaminated" by hearing any foreign language.

Friends and neighbors continued to protest the boy's isolation. And their harassment became even more passionate when four years passed without Ben-Zion speaking a word. All he did was babble. But shortly after his fourth birthday, he spoke his first word — *Abba*, meaning "Father."[41] From that point on he spewed forth a torrent of words and, like his father, he began to make up new words for items around the house![42]

The Hebrew Newspaper

Ben-Yehuda launched the publication of a newspaper shortly after his arrival in Jerusalem, not only because it was part of his master plan, but also because he needed the income to survive. The general population in Jerusalem liked the paper. They had never seen anything like it in the Hebrew language. The settlers in the agricultural villages scattered across Palestine loved it. But the Orthodox were determined to destroy it and tried to do so on several occasions.

To publish the paper, Ben-Yehuda had to constantly create new words. His first challenge was to come up with a word for "newspaper." The word used in Jerusalem was *michtav-et*, which literally meant, "a letter of the time." Ben-Yehuda considered this term to be clumsy, so he took the Hebrew word for "time" and, improvising a bit, he came up with the new word, *itton*, which received public acceptance.[43]

Other words for which he had to manufacture new Hebrew words were soldier, airplane, sport, doll, ice-cream, jelly, omelette, handkerchief, towel, bicycle — and hundreds more.[44]

Sometimes his new words were rejected. One such word was the one he introduced for "tomato." The commonly used word already in circulation was *agbanit*, taken from a root word that meant "to love sensuously." Ben-Yehuda thought that was inappropriate, so he coined the word, *badurah*. The Hebrew speakers stuck with *agbanit*.[45]

Ben-Yehuda was a purist. He would never just transfer a word like "telegraph" into the Hebrew language via a transliteration. No, the new word had to be based on a root Hebrew word.[46]

The Opposition

Opposition to Ben-Yehuda's efforts never let up during his lifetime. The Orthodox were unrelenting in their efforts to prevent their holy language from becoming a secular tongue.[47]

At one point, the Ashkenazic leadership went to the Ottoman rulers and accused Ben-Yehuda of treason, based upon a passage in his newspaper which they had purposefully mistranslated. This resulted in his arrest, trial and conviction. And although he was released on bail, pending an appeal, he was prohibited from publishing his newspaper. He was delivered from this ordeal by Baron Edmond de Rothschild (1845-1934), a French philanthropist and supporter of Zionism, who paid bribes to the prosecutors and judges.[48] During this legal crisis, Ben-Yehuda and his family were formally excommunicated by the Ashkenazic leaders.[49]

Opposition from secular Jews was not so passionate, but it was also persistent. It came mainly in the form of a lack of interest. After all, most of the Jews who formed the nucleus of the Zionist Movement in the 1890s and early 20th Century were Humanists, Socialists, or Communists, and most were Atheists or Agnostics. They had no interest in speaking a biblical language.

Theodor Herzl (1860-1904), considered to be the father of Zionism, is a good example. He was a thoroughly secular person. He considered Hebrew to be "unfeasible," and preferred German instead.[50] Other Zionists advocated Yiddish.

Ben Yehuda was a great admirer of Herzl and traveled to meet him personally several times, but he could never seem to catch up with him. He finally was able to meet Herzl in 1898 when he came to Palestine to confer with Kaiser Wilhelm II during the German leader's visit to the Holy Land. Herzl showed a complete lack of interest in Ben-Yehuda's ideas. That evening, Herzl wrote in his diary:[51]

> I also met a young fanatic who tried to convince me that what our movement needs is to adopt Hebrew as our national language. It is, of course, ridiculous!

The Two Faithful Wives

Throughout all the stress and strain of living in a harsh environment while battling a deadly disease and fighting constant battles to achieve what seemed to be an impossible task, Ben-Yehuda was supported and constantly encouraged by two remarkable wives.

The first was D'vorah who bore him five children while helping him edit his newspaper. She suffered quietly as she was scorned by neighbors and barely had enough money to put food on the table. Ben-Yehuda always referred to her as "the first Hebrew mother in two thousand years" because she was the first to give birth to children who grew up speaking Hebrew as their native language.[52]

D'vorah contracted her husband's tuberculosis and died rather suddenly in 1891 at the age of 37. Ben-Yehuda's words of honor for her, which he published a week later in his newspaper, consisted simply of a quote from Jeremiah 2:2 — "I remember you, the kindness of your youth, the love of your espousals, when you went after me in the wilderness, in a land that was not sown" (Ben-Yehuda's translation).[53]

Ben-Yehuda's grief was compounded two months later when his three youngest children died during a flu epidemic.[54] He was 33 years old, and he desperately needed consolation and help.

Once again, the help came from the Jonas family. Shortly before her death, D'vorah had written to her younger sister, Paula, asking her to take her place as Ben-Yehuda's wife.[55] Solomon Jonas and his wife were appalled by the request since they considered it to be a death warrant for another daughter. But like her older sister, Paula could not be deterred. She had always loved Ben-Yehuda, and she considered it her destiny to take her sister's place and assist him in the accomplishment of his monumental task. She was only 19 years old, so her entire family decided to go with her and immigrate to Palestine![56]

Paula wrote to Ben-Yehuda with the news and requested that he send her a list of possible Hebrew names for herself. Like her sister, she desired to change her name. Ben-Yehuda sent the list and she picked the name of Hemda, not because she liked the way it sounded, but because of its meaning: "beloved or cherished."[57]

Hemda proved to be every bit as faithful, resourceful, supportive and helpful as D'vorah had been. During her 30 years with Ben-Yehuda (1892-1922). She bore him 6 children. She toured all of Europe several times raising financial support for his research and writings. And she was the one who found a prestigious German publisher for his dictionary.

The Hebrew Dictionary

One of Ben-Yehuda's greatest achievements was his creation of a dictionary of the Hebrew language. He began the project by creating a new word for "dictionary." The expression people had been using was *sefer millim*, which meant "book of words." He shortened this to one word, *millon*.[58]

Ben-Yehuda spent most of his life searching for ancient Hebrew words that had been lost. He also sought to find the origin of words and examples of their usage, as well as their changes in meaning throughout the centuries. He scoured libraries all over Europe and the Middle East. And when he moved to the United States during World War I to escape Turkish persecution, he spent four years searching the great libraries of this nation which were located in the Northeast.[59]

When he fled Palestine in 1914, he had already accumulated about 450,000 notes. He packed them up and turned them over to the American consulate in Jerusalem for safekeeping.[60] Those notes were taken from over 40,000 books he had consulted that had been written over a period of more than two thousand years.[61]

What he sought to produce was much more that what we think of as a dictionary. His goal was no less than an encyclopedia of the Hebrew language. He provided definitions of each word in Hebrew, French, German and English. He identified the origin of each word and provided its sister words in other Semitic languages. He provided synonyms and antonyms. He traced the changes in the meaning of the word through the centuries. And he provided overwhelming examples of the use of the word in sentences to help the reader see how to use the word in conversations.[62] For example, the dictionary provided 335 expressions for the word *lo*, which means "no," and 210 for *ken*, which means "yes."[63]

The first volume, published in 1908, covered only the letters *aleph* and *beth*.[64] There are 22 letters in the Hebrew alphabet, of which five have different forms when used at the end of a word.

Ben-Yehuda's Triumph

By 1917, Ben-Yehuda had made such progress on his dictionary and with his effort to resurrect spoken Hebrew from the dead, that he changed the motto on his wall to read: "My day is long; my work is blessed."[65]

Later that year, a dream of his came true. The British issued the Balfour Declaration in November, proclaiming their intention after the war to make Palestine a home for the Jewish people. The next month the city of Jerusalem fell to the Allied Forces, liberating the city from 400 years of Turkish rule.

Ben-Yehuda responded to these momentous events with a paraphrase of Psalm 126: "T'was like a dream when the Lord restored Zion from its bondage."[66]

His greatest victory came in 1921 when the British government recognized three official languages for Palestine: English, Arabic and Hebrew. Postage stamps were issued in Hebrew for the first time ever, anywhere in the world.

By 1922 five volumes of his dictionary had been published, and he had finished writing volumes 6 and 7. His work had received worldwide acclaim.

On December 14, 1922 he finished working on the word *nefesh*," meaning "soul" or "spirit." The next day was Friday, Sabbath eve and the second day of Hanukkah. He told his wife that the next word he would be working on meant "take a breath," and he took that as a word from the Lord that he should take the day off and rest over the Sabbath.[67]

He spent the day walking around his beloved city of Jerusalem. When he returned home, he turned pale and his breathing became labored. He laid down on a sofa to rest, and his wife sent word for doctors. Before long the word had spread all over Jerusalem that he was seriously ill, and the house quickly filled with doctors, city officials and friends.

Ben-Yehuda seemed to have drifted into a coma, but he suddenly raised up on an elbow, looked around the room and said, "Speak Hebrew!" Later, he called for his wife. She asked him if he felt better. His reply was, "Hebrew makes me rest."[68] Those were his last words. He was 64 years old.

Hebrew Today

Ben-Yehuda's wife, Hemda, and her son, Ehud, worked together with linguistic experts to complete the dictionary. It ran a total of 17 volumes and was not completed until 1958, seven years after her death in 1951 at the age of 78.[69]

In the process of compiling his dictionary, Ben-Yehuda had realized there was a need for a group of linguistic experts to help him form new words and to serve as a monitor for the usage of the language. Also, there would be a need to keep his dictionary updated. He therefore formed a group in 1890 which he called The Hebrew Language Committee.[70] It continues to operate to this day as the Academy of the Hebrew Language of the Hebrew University of Jerusalem. It averages the creation of 2,000 new Hebrew words each year.[71]

Also during his lifetime, Ben-Yehuda had developed an intensive method of teaching Hebrew in which only Hebrew was used. It was so effective that his second wife became proficient in the language in only six months.[72] That method is still used today in what are called "ulpan schools." There are approximately 220 of these schools in Israel today teaching over 25,000 students, most of them new immigrants.[73]

There are nearly 200 book publishers in Israel today, and each of them is releasing between 5 and 150 new Hebrew language books per year.[74] An Israeli writer, S. Y. Agnon (1888-1970) was awarded the Nobel Prize in literature in 1966 for his Hebrew language novels.[75]

As of 2013, there were about 9 million Hebrew speakers worldwide, of whom 7 million spoke it fluently.[76]

Conclusion

Ben-Yehuda's grave is situated on the lower slope of the Mount of Olives in Jerusalem. The words on his tombstone read:[77]

> Eliezer Ben-Yehuda, reviver of the Hebrew tongue and composer of the great dictionary. Dead in Jerusalem on the 26th day of Kislev in the sixth year of the Balfour Declaration.

Looking back on his life, the greatest miracle may not have been his revival of Hebrew as a spoken language. Rather, it may well have been God's preservation of his life for 41 years after he was told he had only six months to live.

Eliezer Ben-Yehuda was one of the early pioneers of modern day Israel who gave the new state its language. Many other pioneers combined their efforts to make the land inhabitable. This story is contained in the next chapter.

Chapter 8

The Reclamation of the Land of Israel

As we saw in chapter 4, when the Jews started returning to their homeland in the 1890s, they did not find a land "flowing with milk and honey." Instead, they were faced with trying to eke out a living in a desolate wasteland plagued with malaria-infested swamps. They paid exorbitant prices for the land, and the Arabs who lived there (people who considered themselves to be either Syrians or Turks) laughed all the way to the bank.

But God had promised that when the Jews returned, He would cause their land to be rejuvenated, transforming it from desolation to abundance.

The Prophetic Promises

Isaiah foretold that a day would come when the "Lord will comfort Zion" by restoring her "waste places" and making "her wilderness . . . like Eden and her desert like the garden of the LORD" (Isaiah 51:3). Isaiah proceeded to wax eloquent by saying that when this occurs, "joy and gladness will be found [in the land]" together with "thanksgiving and the sound of a melody" (Isaiah 51:3).

Isaiah also prophesied specifically about the replanting of the forests and the provision of water to the desert. Quoting the Lord, he wrote (Isaiah 41:18-19):

> 18) "I will open rivers on the bare heights and springs in the midst of the valleys; I will make the wilderness a pool of water and the dry land fountains of water.
>
> 19) "I will put the cedar in the wilderness, the acacia and the myrtle and the olive tree; I will place the juniper in the desert together with the box tree and the cypress . . ."

And for what purpose will the Lord do this? Isaiah states it will be done so that the Jewish people "may see and recognize and consider and gain insight . . . that thc hand of the LORD has done this, and the Holy One of Israel has created it" (Isaiah 41:20).

The most detailed prophecy concerning the reclamation of the land is to be found in Ezekiel 36:8-12 where the Lord tells the prophet specifically to "prophesy concerning the land of Israel:"

> 8) "But you, O mountains of Israel, you will put forth your branches and bear your fruit for My people Israel; for they will soon come.
>
> 9) "For, behold, I am for you, and I will turn to you, and you will be cultivated and sown.
>
> 10) "I will multiply men on you, all the house of Israel, all of it; and the cities will be inhabited and the waste places will be rebuilt.
>
> 11) "I will multiply on you man and beast; and they will increase and be fruitful; and I will cause you to be inhabited as you were formerly and will treat you better than at the first. Thus you will know that I am the LORD.
>
> 12) "Yes, I will cause men — My people Israel — to walk on you and possess you, so

> that you will become their inheritance and never again bereave them of children."

Ezekiel sums up his prophecies concerning the restoration in two verses that are astounding (Ezekiel 36:34-35):

> 34) "The desolate land will be cultivated instead of being a desolation in the sight of everyone who passes by.
>
> 35) They will say, 'This desolate land has become like the garden of Eden; and the waste, desolate and ruined cities are fortified and inhabited.'"

"Like the Garden of Eden"! And just like Isaiah, Ezekiel says the result will be that both Jews and Gentiles will come to realize that the Lord is faithful to fulfill His prophetic promises (Ezekiel 36:36).

Reclaiming the Land

When the Jewish people began returning to their homeland in the early 1900s, they organized themselves into fortress-like communities called either a kibbutz or a moshav.[1] These were collective farms that provided mutual help to their members and protection from Arab attacks.

The pioneers went to work immediately, attempting to drain the swamps and get rid of the malaria infested mosquitos. Eucalyptus trees were imported from Australia and planted around the perimeters of the swamps.[2] They were selected because of their reputation for absorbing large amounts of water. When these proved insufficient, canals were dug to drain the swamps to the sea.[3]

At the same time, the pioneers began replanting the forests of Israel. This was a very serious need. From the Sea of Galilee to the south, all the trees had been cut down. In the Galilee area in the north, there were only 15,000 trees left.[4]

The trees had been cut for firewood and military use, and some forests had been burned for hunting purposes.[5] The last sizeable remnants of forests had been cut down in the early 20th Century to fire Turkish railway engines.[6] It is also interesting to note that the Turks taxed trees, so there was an incentive to cut down trees to alleviate the tax burden![7]

As the trees were being planted and the land cleared of rocks so that it could be recultivated, the rainfall began to increase miraculously. During the 20th Century, it increased 10 percent every decade, for a total increase of over 100 percent![8]

The JNF

The key to the reclamation of the land of Israel proved to be an amazing organization called The Jewish National Fund.[9] It was established at the Fifth Zionist Congress in Basel, Switzerland in 1901. Its sole purpose was to acquire and develop land for Jewish occupation.

In addition to relying on wealthy donors, the JNF raised money in a down-to-earth way by distributing collection boxes to Jewish homes. These came to be known as "The Blue Boxes." During the period between the two world wars, about one million of these tin collection boxes were distributed to Jewish homes throughout the world.[10] From 1902 to the late 1940s, the JNF also sold colorful stamps to raise money.[11]

The JNF bought its first parcel of land in 1903. It consisted of 50 acres in Hadera, located on the Mediterranean coast, about 25 miles north of Tel Aviv.[12] The organization played a central role in the establishment of the first modern Jewish city — Tel Aviv in 1909.[13] By 1927, the JNF had purchased a total of over 50,000 acres of land on which 50 communities stood.[14] By the eve of statehood in May 1948, the JNF had acquired 231,290 acres of land.[15]

The record of accomplishments of the JNF by the beginning of the 21st Century was truly remarkable. The organization owned 13 percent of the total land in Israel, and it had built 180 dams and reservoirs, developed 25,000 acres of land and established more than 1,000 parks.[16]

Reforestation

One of the major projects of the JNF throughout its history has been reforestation. The Bible itself has often served as the guide. For example, one of Israel's foremost authorities on reforestation remembered that Abraham planted tamarisk trees in Beersheba, located in the southern Negev Desert area. Following Abraham's lead, over 2 million of the trees were planted in the same area, and it was determined that the tamarisk really does thrive in areas of scanty rainfall.[17]

One of the JNF's most amazing accomplishments during the 20th Century was the planting of more than 240 million trees (and I personally planted at least 100 of them!).[18] Israel was one of only two nations in the world to enter the 21st Century with a net gain of trees.[19]

The planting of so many trees curbed the erosion of the soil, contributed to an increase of oxygen in the atmosphere and provided a natural habitat for wild animals and birds.

Water Conservation

The conservation and distribution of water has also played a key role in Israel's reclamation of its land. The major need was to devise a method to transfer water from the Sea of Galilee in the north to the major cities in the south and to the Negev Desert in the extreme south.

In 1953 construction began on a water carrier that would transport water from the Sea of Galilee to the Negev Desert in a complex system of giant pipes, open canals, tunnels, reservoirs and mammoth pumping stations. The National

Water Carrier was inaugurated in 1964, with 80 percent of its water being allocated to agriculture and 20 percent for drinking water.[20]

Another key element was the development of drip irrigation whereby flexible water pipes were spread out on the ground with holes in them to distribute the precious water at the base of each plant. This innovation stopped the waste of water that occurred through evaporation when irrigation was done by spraying water into the air.[21]

As immigrants have continued to flood into Israel over the years, the demand for water has greatly increased. The situation reached a crisis point in 2008 after a decade-long drought. Israel's largest source of fresh water, the Sea of Galilee, had dropped within inches of the "black line" at which point irrevocable salt infiltration would flood the lake and ruin it permanently.[22]

Severe water rationing was imposed and low-flow toilets and shower heads were installed nationwide. Additionally, water treatment systems were developed that recaptured 86 percent of used water for irrigation — vastly more than the second most efficient country in the world, Spain, which recycles 19 percent.[23]

In 2009 the situation began to turn around due to the construction of desalination plants designed to convert sea water into fresh water. The first had opened in 2005 in Ashkelon, on the Mediterranean coast, 30 miles south of Tel Aviv. The second started operating in 2009 at Hadera, located on the coast about 25 miles north of Tel Aviv. The largest in the world, the Sorek Plant, opened in 2013 and is located ten miles south of Tel Aviv.[24] It is capable of producing seven million gallons of potable water every hour![25]

Desalination currently provides 785 million cubic yards of water per year — an amazing 55% percent of the nation's water needs.[26]

Agriculture

The result of all these reclamation efforts has been phenomenal. The land that was desolate at the beginning of the 20th Century is now the bread basket of the Middle East. The nation is now agriculturally self-sufficient except for grain imports.[27] It exports agricultural products to both the Arab countries of the Middle East and to the nations of Europe.

When people think of Jews, they normally think of people who have excelled in the area of finance. But modern Jews in Israel have made their mark in agricultural production, military prowess and, in more recent years, high-tech innovations.

Due to the diversity of the land and climate across the country, and all the efforts at reclamation, Israel is able to grow a wide range of crops. Field crops include wheat, sorghum, corn and cotton. Fruit and vegetables grown include citrus, avocados, kiwi fruit, guavas, mangoes and grapes. Additionally, tomatoes, cucumbers, pepper, zucchini and melons are commonly grown throughout the country. Subtropical areas produce bananas and dates, while in the northern hills, apples, pears and cherries are grown.[28]

The dairies of Israel produce the highest amounts of milk per animal in the world.[29] Israel is one of the world's leading fresh citrus producers and exporters, including oranges, grapefruit and tangerines.[30] The Israelis have developed the world's first long shelf-life commercial tomato varieties.[31] Overall, Israel is the world's leader in agricultural research and development.[32]

Israel produces vast quantities of flowers for export. In fact, Israel produces 5 percent of the world's flowers and is surpassed in production only by the Netherlands and Kenya.[33] The process for picking, packing and distribution is so streamlined that flowers can be delivered to Europe via temperature-controlled jets within two days of their harvest.[34]

Today, Israel is focusing on the greening of the Negev Desert which constitutes 55 percent of the nation's land. They have devised water conservation techniques to save the one inch of rainfall per year in the Negev. They have also genetically engineered plants to grow on the brackish water reservoirs that exist below the surface of the desert. They have even developed a strain of potatoes that thrive in a hot, dry climate like a desert and can be irrigated with salt water.[35]

As a result of these efforts, half a million Jews now live in the desert, in 250 thriving agricultural settlements.[36] The American Society for Horticultural Sciences recently stated that Israel's desert agricultural technology is "one of the most significant advances in food production in the past 1,000 years."[37] Today, over 10,000 Israeli brackish water specialists are training agronomists and farmers in 54 countries around the world.[38]

Perhaps the most amazing thing that can be said about the reclamation of the land and the agriculture it has produced is that the United Nations, which normally specializes in condemning Israel, has declared that Israel is "the most agriculturally efficient land on earth."[39]

Prophecy Fulfilled

Can there be any doubt that Ezekiel's astounding prophecy about the reclamation of the land of Israel in the end times has been fulfilled? Read it again (Ezekiel 36:34-35):

> 34) "The desolate land will be cultivated instead of being a desolation in the sight of everyone who passes by.
>
> 35) They will say, 'This desolate land has become like the garden of Eden; and the waste, desolate and ruined cities are fortified and inhabited.'"

Or consider again this prophecy of Isaiah (Isaiah 51:3):

> Indeed, the LORD will comfort Zion;
> He will comfort all her waste places.
> And her wilderness He will make like Eden,
> And her desert like the garden of the LORD;
> Joy and gladness will be found in her,
> Thanksgiving and sound of a melody.

Can there be any doubt that the detailed fulfillment of these prophecies proves that God is on the throne and that He is in control of history? Can there be any doubt that He has a very specific purpose for the Jewish People in the end times? And can there be any doubt that God is going to accomplish all His purposes among the Jewish people?

Chapter 9

The Resurgence of the Israeli Military

Let's take an in-depth look now at a fifth prophecy concerning Israel in the end times that was fulfilled in the 20th Century and continues to be fulfilled to this day — the resurgence of the Israeli military.

When I refer to "resurgence," I have in mind the fact that the Jewish people were a formidable military force in Bible times, as long as they were operating in the center of God's will. They established a reputation for military power the moment they entered their Promised Land when they overthrew the city of Jericho. They continued to conquer the whole land in victory after victory, including the Jebusite city of Jerusalem, which they made their capital.

Many of their military victories were very miraculous, as when Deborah and Barak defeated the armies of the Canaanites in the Valley of Jezreel at the base of Mount Tabor (Judges 4). Or when Gideon, with only 300 men, was able to defeat the combined armies of the Midianites and the Amalekites by attacking them in the middle of the night (Judges 7).

The military power of the Israelites was consolidated under the reigns of David and Solomon. After the kingdom split, following the death of Solomon, the southern nation of Judah continued to excel militarily, including miraculous victories like the one when King Jehoshaphat defeated the combined armies of the Moabites and the Ammonites by sending forth an army led by singers and dancers and worship leaders! This strange collection of "soldiers" so befuddled the enemy that they fell into total confusion and were then ambushed and routed (2 Chronicles 20).

The prophet Ezekiel prophesied that the revival of Israel in the last days would produce "an exceedingly great army" (Ezekiel 37: 10).

Zechariah was more specific. He prophesied that God would make "the clans of Judah like a firepot among pieces of wood and a flaming torch among sheaves," enabling them to "consume on the right hand and on the left" all their enemies (Zechariah 12:6). He proceeded to state that in the end times, the nation would be so strong that the "feeble among them in that day will be like David, and the house of David will be like God, like the angel of the Lord before them" (Zechariah 12:8).

Let's look now at the evidence of the fulfillment of these prophecies.

The War of Independence (November 1947 - March 1949)

On November 29, 1947 the United Nations adopted a resolution providing for the ending of the League of Nations Mandate for Palestine, replacing British rule with a partition of the land that would result in the creation of two states, one for the Jews and the other for the Arabs.

The Jews worldwide were elated, even though the piece of territory they were provided was minuscule compared to what they had been promised by the British in the Balfour Declaration in November of 1917. But the Arabs were outraged because they wanted all the land of Palestine. The result was the immediate launching of a wave of terrorism as the Arabs began to attack Jewish communities. This bloody conflict continued right up to the day that the Jews issued their declaration of independence on May 14, 1948.

As that epic day approached, the Arabs issued repeated warnings that they would launch an all-out war if the Jews proceeded to establish a state. For example, the Secretary General of the Arab League, Azzam Pasha, declared, "It will be a war of annihilation. It will be a momentous massacre in history that will be talked about like the massacres of the Mongols or the Crusades."[1]

On the Jewish side, there was considerable concern that such boasting could become a reality. Thus, on the eve of the war, Yigael Yadin, the Chief of Staff of the Israeli forces, told David Ben-Gurion, the Jewish leader, "The best we can tell you is that we have a 50-50 chance." [2]

The trepidation on the part of the Jews was more than justified. Within hours of the declaration of independence on the afternoon of May 14, 1948, five Arab armies began invading the new nation (Egypt, Syria, Transjordan, Lebanon and Iraq). The Israeli forces consisted at most of 30,000 rag-tag underground fighters who were ill-trained and poorly equipped. (The Israeli Defense Force, known as the IDF, was not organized until after the invasion.)

The Arab armies, particularly the Jordanians, were well equipped and trained. Egypt, Iraq and Syria had air forces. Egypt and Syria also had tank forces. All had modern artillery.[3] The troops of Transjordan were led by a British officer, General John Glubb.

Although the United States recognized the new state of Israel immediately, the Truman Administration did not provide any aid. Instead, Truman declared an arms embargo under the naive assumption that it would help avert bloodshed. Meanwhile, the British gladly supplied arms openly to the Arabs, while Israel had to smuggle weapons purchased in Czechoslovakia.

But despite the overwhelming odds against them, the infant Jewish state prevailed. The cost was enormous. A total of 6,377 Israelis were killed, representing nearly one percent of the population (equivalent to an American loss today of three million!).

However, the Israelis ended up not only with the territory that had been allotted to them by the UN, but also with control of 60% of the area that had been proposed for an Arab state. Arab casualties totaled between 8,000 and 15,000, and they ended up with only 22% of the total territory of Palestine.[4]

The only key area that the Israelis were unable to conquer was the Old City of Jerusalem. Overall, the war resulted in an incredible, miraculous victory for Israel.

The Story of Yad Mordechai

During the war there were many miraculous events. One occurred at a kibbutz (collective farm) called Yad Mordechai, located 36 miles south of Tel Aviv near the northern border of the Gaza Strip. The kibbutz was located on the coastal road from Egypt to Tel Aviv.

The Egyptian army, composed of 5,000 troops, divided as it moved north. Half the troops headed for Jerusalem, the other 2,500 continued north toward Tel Aviv. The latter unit arrived at Yad Mordechai on May 19. They were heavily armed, and they were backed up with tanks, artillery and air support.[5]

The kibbutz evacuated all its children and most of its women as they prepared for the Egyptian attack. They were left with 130 defenders (110 kibbutzniks and 20 fighters from Tel Aviv). They dug trenches and reinforced them with sand bags. Their armament consisted of 37 rifles, one anti-tank gun, two light mortars and two machine guns.[6]

There was no hope for the kibbutz, and its defenders were well aware of that fact. But they bravely dug in and prepared to take what appeared to be a suicidal stand.

The Egyptians attacked furiously with ground troops, tank assaults, artillery barrages, and air sorties. Incredibly, the Yad Mordechai defenders held out for five days! The Egyptians were not able to overrun the kibbutz until the defenders decided to retreat under the cover of darkness due to the fact that half of them had either been killed or incapacitated.[7]

Over 300 Egyptian soldiers died in the battle, and the five days gave the defenders of Tel Aviv time to prepare their defenses. Also, during that time, four Messerschmitt airplanes had arrived in crates from Czechoslovakia and had been hastily assembled. They were used on May 29 to stop the Egyptian army before it could reach Tel Aviv.[8]

How could 130 untrained civilians with only rudimentary armament hold off the Egyptian army for five days? No one has ever been able to explain it.

The Six Day War (June 1967)

In the early 1960s, Gamal Abdel Nasser, the President of Egypt, decided to try to establish his nation as the leader of the Arab world. Part of that strategy was the demonization of Israel in his public speeches. He also encouraged terrorist attacks against Israel.

In 1965 Nasser asserted, "We shall not enter Palestine with its soil covered in sand; we shall enter it with its soil saturated in blood."[9] A few months later, Nasser declared that he had two aims. "The immediate aim: perfection of Arab military might. The national aim: the eradication of Israel."[10]

On May 15, 1967, Nasser started moving Egyptian troops into the Sinai desert, massing them near the Israeli border. He then ordered the UN troops in the buffer zone between Israel and Egypt to leave. When the UN readily complied, he announced:[11]

> As of today, there no longer exists an international emergency force to protect Israel.

> We shall exercise patience no more. We shall not complain any more to the UN about Israel. The sole method we shall apply against Israel is total war, which will result in the extermination of Zionist existence.

The Syrian Defense Minister, Hafez Assad, replied enthusiastically: "The Syrian army, with its finger on the trigger, is united . . . [and] I, as a military man, believe that the time has come to enter into a battle of annihilation."[12]

On May 22, Egypt blockaded the Straits of Tiran to all Israeli shipping — an action considered to be an act of war under international law. At that point, Nasser began to challenge Israel daily to fight. On May 28, he declared, "We will not accept any . . . coexistence with Israel."[13]

King Hussein of Jordan signed a defense pact with Egypt on May 30, and Nasser announced:[14]

> The armies of Egypt, Jordan, Syria and Lebanon are poised on the borders of Israel, while standing behind us are the armies of Iraq, Algeria, Kuwait, Sudan and the whole Arab nation . . . the critical hour has arrived. We have reached the stage of serious action and not declarations.

President Abdur Rahman Aref of Iraq joined in the war of words, declaring, "Our goal is clear — to wipe Israel off the map."[15]

The Arab rhetoric was matched by the mobilization of forces. Approximately 465,000 troops, together with 2,800 tanks and 800 aircraft were assembled for the attack on Israel.[16]

The Attack

The Israeli leaders decided it would be suicidal to wait for the attack, and so, on June 5, Prime Minister Levi Eshkol gave the order to launch a preemptive attack on Egypt. The entire Israeli Air Force, with the exception of 12 planes assigned to defend Israel's air space, took off in the early morning, and in less than two hours they destroyed over 300 Egyptian aircraft sitting on the ground. A few hours later, they destroyed all the Jordanian air force and half of Syria's on the ground.[17]

These overwhelmingly successful surprise attacks guaranteed an Israeli victory before the ground war could get started.

After just six days of fighting, the Israeli forces on the ground had captured the Sinai, the Gaza Strip, the West Bank and the Golan Heights. Most important, they were able to conquer the Old City of Jerusalem and regain control of the sacred Temple Mount.

After breaking into the Old City, the Israeli troops rushed to the Western Wall of the Temple Mount to pray. No Jew had been allowed access to that area for 18 years, ever since the Jordanians had taken the city in the War of Independence.

Rabbi Shlomo Goren, the chief rabbi of Israel's army (and later the chief rabbi of Israel) rushed to the wall. He had a torah scroll under one arm and a shofar in the other hand. He blew the shofar and announced: "We have taken the City of God. We are entering the Messianic era for the Jewish people."[18] He said that because he knew from prophecies in the Hebrew scriptures that when the Jews are back in the land and back in their capital city, the Messiah will come.

Once again, the tiny nation of Israel had prevailed against unbeatable odds, just as prophesied in the ancient Hebrew scriptures. The victory had been achieved with lightning swiftness, in only six days, proving to be one of the most miraculous wars in history.

The Yom Kippur War (October 1973)

The situation proved to be quite different in 1973 when the Arabs enjoyed the element of surprise. Egypt and Syria launched an all-out surprise attack against Israel on October 6, which happened to be Yom Kippur, the holiest day on the Jewish calendar.

The Egyptians suddenly crossed the Suez Canal, quickly overran the Israeli outposts along the canal, and then drove deep into the Sinai before the Israelis could mobilize their forces, deploy them, and launch a counter-attack. Meanwhile, the Syrians had simultaneously attacked the Golan Heights.

The war was prompted by a desire on the part of the Egyptian President, Anwar Sadat, to avenge the humiliation the Arab world had suffered in the 1967 Six Day War. Although Sadat warned repeatedly in 1971, 1972 and 1973 that he was going to renew the war with Israel, most observers remained skeptical.

It was not until a few hours before the attack began that the Israeli Chief of Staff, David Elazar, recommended a full, immediate mobilization and a preemptive air strike. But he was overruled by Prime Minister Golda Meir who feared that striking first would anger the United States and motivate President Nixon to refuse to support Israel.[19]

The news of the attack also caught the U.S. by surprise because the very day before, the CIA had reported to President Nixon "that war in the Middle East is unlikely."[20]

Once again, as in all its previous wars, Israel faced overwhelming odds:[21]

> On the Golan Heights, approximately 180 Israeli tanks faced an onslaught of 1,400 Syrian tanks. Along the Suez Canal, fewer than 500 Israelis defenders with only 3 tanks were attacked by 600,000 Egyptian soldiers,

backed by 2,000 tanks and 550 aircraft.

Furthermore, at least nine Arab states provided aid to the Egyptian-Syrian war effort, including Saudi Arabia and Kuwait who served as the financial underwriters. Most importantly, the Soviet Union was heavily involved, providing military supplies, intelligence and diplomatic support.

In short, it appeared that Israel had no hope. They had been blind-sided on their holiest day of the year, and they were greatly out-manned and out-gunned.

The Israeli Victory

Israel prevailed because of massive aid from the Nixon Administration and because of brilliant generalship in the marshalling of its armies.

The U.S. supplied $2.2 billion in emergency aid that totaled 22,000 tons of equipment that was transported to Israel in 566 flights.[22]

The Israeli military leaders utilized this aid to stop the Syrians dead in their tracks on the Golan Heights, while General Ariel Sharon led the Israeli tank forces in the Sinai in a counter-attack that resulted in the greatest tank battle in history.

By October 15 (only 9 days after the war had started), the Egyptian tank force had been destroyed, and Sharon had crossed the Suez Canal. He quickly surrounded the Egyptian Third Army, immobilized it, and started marching toward Cairo.

Meanwhile, in the north, the Israeli forces had cleared the Golan Heights, recaptured Mount Hermon and had started driving toward Damascus.

Israeli forces were 25 miles from Damascus and 63 miles from Cairo when the Soviets decided to pressure the United Nations into calling for a cease fire.

Once again, Israel had prevailed when there seemed to be no hope.

Operation Thunderbolt (July 1976)

On June 27, 1976 an Air France flight from Tel Aviv to Paris made a stopover in Athens where it unloaded some passengers and picked up others. Among those who got on the flight were four terrorists, two Palestinians and two Germans. They hijacked the flight as soon as it took off, and they then diverted it to Benghazi, Libya where it was refueled. From there they headed to Entebbe, Uganda where the President of the country, Idi Amin, was waiting to welcome them.[23]

Upon landing, four more terrorists joined the group, and they proceeded to separate the hostages. All the Jews were herded into a recently abandoned terminal building. The rest of the passengers were released and flown to Paris. The Air France crew decided to stay behind with the Jewish hostages. The number of hostages, including the crew, totaled 106.

The hijackers immediately issued an ultimatum: Either release 53 terrorists held in Israel and four in other countries, or all the hostages would be killed on July 1.

The Israeli government launched negotiations with the terrorists while considering a military alternative. As a result of the negotiations, the hijackers agreed to extend the deadline to July 4.

A military alternative was considered by most to be unthinkable, mainly because of the great distance involved — 2,500 miles from Tel Aviv to Entebbe. Nonetheless, the Israeli Cabinet ordered the preparation of a rescue mission while they used the negotiations to stall for time.

As it turned out, the Israelis had two advantages working for them. They were able to interview all the passengers who had been released, and from them they got detailed information about the captors and the hostages. They also discovered that the abandoned terminal building had been built by an Israeli company, so they were able to get the blueprints of the building!

Lieutenant Colonel Jonathan (Yoni) Netanyahu was selected to lead the commando assault team. He was the older brother of the man who would later become the prime minister of Israel — Benjamin Netanyahu.

Although Yoni was only 30 years old, he had accumulated an outstanding record of military leadership and daring. To prepare his team for the attack, he came up with the idea of using hay bales to lay out the exact floor plan of the terminal building, and his commando team began practicing mock assaults.

The Raid

Four Lockheed C-130 Hercules aircraft, plus two Boeing 747s were used in the raid. More than 100 personnel were recruited and divided into teams.

Yoni's assault group consisted of 29 elite commandos. A second group was assigned the job of encircling the new terminal building and immobilizing the Ugandan soldiers attached to it. A further group was given the task of destroying all the MiG fighter planes on the ground at the airport. A fourth group was assigned the responsibility of refueling the airplanes, and a fifth squad was put in charge of rounding up and evacuating the hostages.

The mission was launched on the afternoon of July 3. The planes flew most of the way at an altitude of only 100 feet in order to avoid radar detection. The flight took 7 hours and 40 minutes. They arrived one minute behind schedule — just after midnight in Uganda, the beginning of July 4, 1976.

The surprise blitz attack proved successful beyond any expectations. It took a total of only 53 minutes. During that time, all seven of the hijackers who were present were killed, together with 33 to 45 Ugandan soldiers, and all 8 MiG fighter planes on the ground were destroyed.[24]

Three hostages died in the crossfire, and ten were wounded. One was left behind because she had been taken to a hospital in Entebbe. A total of 102 hostages were taken back to Israel alive.[25]

Five Israeli commandos were wounded. Only one was killed — the leader of the raid, Yoni Netanyahu.

The entire raid, including the refueling of the planes and the evacuation of the hostages, took a total of only one hour and 39 minutes.[26] To this day, this amazing raid is considered to be one of the most outstanding examples of military planning, coordination and execution in the annals of military history.

Operation Opera (June 1981)

In 1976 Iraq purchased an "Osiris-class" nuclear reactor from France. The site chosen for the reactor was about 10 miles southeast of Baghdad. It was given the name of Osirak.

While both France and Iraq claimed that the Osirak reactor was for peaceful scientific research, the Israelis viewed the whole project with great suspicion. When both American and Israeli intelligence sources confirmed Iraq's intention to use the reactor to develop nuclear weapons, the Israelis launched an intensive diplomatic effort to try to halt the French financial and scientific support for the project, but all diplomatic efforts failed.[27]

In early 1981 when the Israeli Cabinet received word that a shipment of 90 kilograms of enriched uranium fuel rods was expected to be supplied by France any moment, they decided, under the leadership of Prime Minister Menachem Begin, to prepare for an immediate attack.[28] This decision was, of course, prompted by a desire to prevent the reactor from being activated. But it was also motivated by a concern that if the attack occurred after activation, it would pose a radiation threat to the inhabitants of Baghdad.[29]

The Attack

The mission to destroy the Osirak reactor was launched on June 7, 1981. The attack squadron consisted of eight F-16s, each with two 2,000 pound bombs, and six F-15s, which were assigned the task of providing fighter support.[30]

The planes departed from an air force base in the southern Negev desert. They flew over the Gulf of Aqaba, skirted the southern border of Jordan, and flew low over Saudi Arabia to avoid radar detection. Arriving in the late afternoon, they caught the Iraqis by complete surprise and totally destroyed the reactor in an attack that took less than two minutes. All the Israeli planes returned home safely.

In a weird coincidence, King Hussein of Jordan was vacationing on his yacht in the Gulf of Aqaba at the time. Since the Israeli jets took off from the Etzion airbase in the southern Negev desert, they flew directly over the King's yacht, and when he saw them, he immediately jumped to the conclusion that they were headed to Iraq to bomb the Osirak reactor. He called his office in Amman and asked them to send an urgent warning to Iraq, but for some unknown reason, the warning was never received by the Iraqis.[31]

Also, it was learned after the attack that half an hour before the Israeli planes arrived, the group of Iraqi soldiers manning the anti-aircraft defenses for the reactor had left their posts for an afternoon meal, and they had turned off their radar detectors.[32]

The leader of the attack force, Ze'ev Raz, was interviewed in 2007 by the *Jewish Press*. As he was recounting the events, the interviewer said, "The way you are describing it, it sounds like an outright miracle." Raz responded, "Absolutely. Of course it was a miracle. How is it possible that even after we bombed the reactor not one plane tried to down us?" He then continued with an amazing observation:[33]

> I'll tell you something else: It takes an hour and a half to get back from Iraq to Israel and we were flying 40,000 feet above the ground. The General Staff originally wanted us to carry out the bombing after sunset so it would be harder for the Iraqis to attack us on the way back.
>
> But I was opposed to that. I thought if we did the bombing after sunset there wouldn't be enough light and our planes would miss their target — so I insisted that the bombing take place before sunset.
>
> As a result, we flew back as the sun was setting. But since the planes were traveling at such a fast speed, the sun was out all the time and never set. It was as though it remained standing in the middle of the horizon.
>
> At that time we pilots all radioed each other reciting the same exact biblical verse — Joshua 10:12: "Sun, stand still over Gibeon, and moon, over the Valley of Ayalon."

God's Protection

I am convinced that the examples cited above prove beyond a doubt that God has His hand on Israel, protecting the Jewish people from assault after assault, and enabling them to achieve miraculous victories — all in fulfillment of Bible prophecies about Israel in the end times.

Nor can there be any doubt that God's supernatural protection will continue for the immediate future.

Currently, a major war looms over the Middle East as Arab secular leaders are being replaced by Muslim fundamentalists who are determined to "liberate" Jerusalem and annihilate Israel. It could well prove to be the worst of all the wars Israel has experienced because missiles are going to rain down on the nation from all directions.

But if Psalm 83 is a prophecy about this war, as I think it could well be, then Israel will once again be overwhelmingly victorious, defeating all the Arab nations with whom it shares a common border. This will pave the way for the subsequent war of Gog and Magog, described in Ezekiel 38 and 39, when Russia, accompanied by certain Muslim nations, will come down against Israel and will suffer supernatural destruction at the hands of the Lord.

Biblical Words of Comfort

Israel has some very difficult days ahead, but God has made some wonderful promises to them that they can rely on. In Psalm 121:4 He says, "Behold, He who keeps Israel will neither slumber nor sleep." In Isaiah 54:17 He promises, "No weapon formed against you shall prosper." And in Joel 3:2 He states that He will severely judge all nations in the end times who get involved in trying to divide up "My land."

Another of God's powerful promises to Israel is found in Isaiah 41:8-16 which reads as follows:

> 8) "But you, Israel, My servant,
> Jacob whom I have chosen,
> Descendant of Abraham My friend,
>
> 9) "You whom I have taken from the ends
> of the earth,
> And called from its remotest parts
> And said to you, 'You are My servant,
> I have chosen you and not rejected you.

10) 'Do not fear, for I am with you;
Do not anxiously look about you, for I am your God.
I will strengthen you, surely I will help you,
Surely I will uphold you with My righteous right hand.'

11) "Behold, all those who are angered at you will be shamed and dishonored;
Those who contend with you will be as nothing and will perish.

12) "You will seek those who quarrel with you, but will not find them,
Those who war with you will be as nothing and non-existent.

13) "For I am the LORD your God, who upholds your right hand,
Who says to you, 'Do not fear, I will help you.'

14) "Do not fear, you worm Jacob, you men of Israel;
I will help you," declares the LORD, "and your Redeemer is the Holy One of Israel.

15) "Behold, I have made you a new, sharp threshing sledge with double edges;
You will thresh the mountains and pulverize them,
And will make the hills like chaff.

16) "You will winnow them, and the wind will carry them away,
And the storm will scatter them;
But you will rejoice in the LORD,
You will glory in the Holy One of Israel."

Our nation needs to pay attention to these promises of God. In recent years, we have put enormous pressure on

Israel to follow a path of appeasement by "trading land for peace." In the process we have increasingly given encouragement to Israel's sworn enemies. If we continue to manhandle Israel, we will end up guaranteeing our own destruction.

Chapter 10

The Re-occupation of the City of Jerusalem

On September 25th of 1995 a very special Jewish new year began. It was the year designated by the government of Israel as the 3,000th anniversary of the conquest of the city of Jerusalem by King David.

The City's Significance

There is no other city on the face of the earth as important as the city of Jerusalem. All the other great cities of the earth — New York, London, Moscow, Paris, and even Rome — pale by comparison. What other city can claim to be "the city of God" or "the city of the Great King"? (Psalm 48).

God loves Jerusalem, and at the beginning of the Eternal State, the Bible says He will take up residence in the city and will live in it eternally, together with His redeemed saints (Revelation 21:1-7). Psalm 68:16 says that God has desired the mountain of Zion "for His abode" and that He intends to "dwell there forever." Psalm 132:13-14 contains a similar promise: "The Lord has chosen Zion; He has desired it for His habitation. 'This is my resting place forever; here I will dwell, for I have desired it.'"

When you read these kind of statements, you can understand why Jerusalem is identified in Ezekiel 5:5 as "the center of the nations" and in Ezekiel 38:12 as "the center of the earth."

Jerusalem is where the Son of God shed His precious blood. It is where Jesus ascended into Heaven. It is where Jesus will return to be crowned King of kings. It is the city from which Jesus will reign over all the nations of the world.

And Jerusalem will be the scene of history's last battle when Satan rallies the nations at the end of the Millennium and leads them in revolt against the Lord. And again, Jerusalem is where God Himself will come to reside eternally with the Redeemed.

It is no wonder that Jerusalem has always been an important topic of Bible prophecy.

The City in History

But before we look at Jerusalem in prophecy, let's briefly remind ourselves of its history.

The first mention of Jerusalem in the Bible is probably found in Genesis 14:18 where we are told that Abraham paid tithes to the King of Salem, Melchizedek. (This was about 2,000 years before the time of Jesus.) Although we cannot know for certain that this is a reference to Jerusalem, it seems likely because Abraham was in that geographical area, and the city's name, Salem, is the root word of the city's later name, Jerusalem.

Later, we are told that Abraham went to Mt. Moriah, just north of ancient Jerusalem, to offer his son, Isaac, as a sacrifice (Genesis 22:2). That mountain was later incorporated into the city of Jerusalem during the time of Solomon, becoming the Temple Mount.

The first mention of the city by the name of Jerusalem is found in Joshua 10:1 where we are told that the city's king, Adonai-zedek, led a coalition of kings against Joshua and was defeated in the famous battle in the Valley of Ayalon when the sun stood still. However, the city of Jerusalem must not have been taken at this time by the Israelites because after the death of Joshua, we are told in Judges 1:8 that "the sons of Judah" captured the city, "struck it with the edge of the sword, and set it on fire."

But the Jebusites must have reclaimed it because it is later referred to in Judges 19:10 as the city of Jebus. And it was still in Jebusite hands two centuries later when David conquered it and made it the capital of the Jewish nation.

The story of the city's capture by David and his forces is recorded in 2 Samuel 5 and 1 Chronicles 11. According to these passages, David reigned from Hebron for seven years while he served as king of Judah. But after he was crowned the king of both Judah and Israel, he decided to move his headquarters northward to a more central location.

The city he selected was Jebus, which was also known as "the stronghold of Zion" (2 Samuel 5:7). After he conquered it, the name was changed to Jerusalem, but it was often referred to as "the city of David" (2 Samuel 5:9). This occurred 1,000 years before the birth of Jesus — or some 3,000 years from where we stand now in human history.

Now, with this brief historical sketch as a backdrop, let's take a look at the Bible prophecies that relate to Jerusalem.

Jewish Jerusalem

The first set of prophecies relating to Jerusalem are those that pertain to it as the Jewish capital before the time of Jesus.

Keep in mind that the kingdom of David split into two nations after the death of his son Solomon. The northern nation of Israel was totally apostate from the beginning. It was given over to idolatry and did not have one righteous king in its 200 year history.

In sharp contrast, the southern nation of Judah was blessed with many righteous kings. It was also blessed with Jerusalem as its capital. And it was blessed even more by having the Shekinah Glory of God residing in its Temple.

But despite all these blessings, the people of Judah became proud and began to drift in their relationship with God. As the nation began to turn its back on God, the Lord mercifully raised up prophets to warn them and call them to repentance. When they refused to repent, the prophets prophesied that the city of Jerusalem would be destroyed and the nation would be taken into captivity.

The first of these prophecies was delivered by Micah in the 8th century BC — about 130 years before the city was actually destroyed. Micah spoke out against both political and religious corruption, saying, "Her [Judah's] leaders pronounce judgment for a bribe, her priests instruct for a price, and her prophets divine for money" (Micah 3:11).

He lamented the fact that every time these leaders were called to repentance lest the city be destroyed, they always responded arrogantly by observing, "Is not the LORD in our midst? [A reference to the Shekinah in the Temple.] Calamity will not come upon us." To which Micah replied: "Therefore, on account of you, Zion will be plowed as a field, Jerusalem will become a heap of ruins, and the mountain of the temple will become high places of a forest" (Micah 3:12).

One hundred years later Jeremiah also warned that Jerusalem would be destroyed (Jeremiah 7:12-15). Speaking for the Lord, Jeremiah declared, "I will make Jerusalem a heap of ruins, a haunt of jackals; and I will make the cities of Judah a desolation, without inhabitant" (Jeremiah 9:11).

When the people refused to believe his words and even sought to kill him as a traitor, Jeremiah reminded them of the previous prophecy of Micah (Jeremiah 26:18). But the people still refused to repent, and the prophecies were fulfilled in 587 BC when Nebuchadnezzer destroyed the city and its temple.

A Second Destruction and Dispersion

After 70 years of captivity in Babylon, the Jews were allowed to return to Jerusalem to rebuild the city and their temple.

But they quickly grew cold in their relationship with the Lord. As a result, they lost interest in rebuilding the temple and started focusing instead on the construction of their own houses. That's when God sent a prophet to call them to repentance and to demand that they get back to work on the temple.

That prophet was Haggai who began to speak out around 520 BC. He pointed out that they had been suffering a series of natural calamities that had ruined their crops, and he asserted that these were remedial judgments from God, calling the people to repentance. "Consider your ways!" he thundered. He pointed out that they were paneling their houses while the "Lord's house lies desolate" (Haggai 1:4-5).

The people repented and went back to work rebuilding the temple, and the Lord responded by sending a prophet with a message of hope to encourage them — a young man named Zechariah. As they worked on the temple, he gave them visions of the Millennial Age when Jerusalem would be returned to all its glory and the Messiah would live in their midst (Zechariah 8).

But the people became discouraged over the pitiful size and beauty of the reconstructed temple, as compared with the First Temple (Ezra 3:10-13). Once again, they began to drift from the Lord, and once again, they began to intermarry with the heathen people in the land (Ezra 9).

In response, God sent another prophet, Malachi, to rebuke the political and spiritual leaders and to call the people to repentance. He denounced them for a divorce epidemic that was raging among them (Malachi 2:13-17). He also condemned them for failing to tithe (Malachi 3:8-10). Speaking through the prophet, the Lord summed up the situation by proclaiming, "From the days of your fathers, you have turned aside from My statutes and have not kept them. Return to Me, and I will return to you" (Malachi 3:7).

But this time, the return did not occur. This, of course, did not surprise the Lord. He had already made it clear through the prophet Daniel that a day was coming when the stubborn disobedience of the Jewish people would result in another destruction of the beloved city and temple.

In Daniel chapter 9, the prophet was given an amazing prophecy about the future of his people and the capital city of Jerusalem. Daniel was told by the Angel Gabriel that God would accomplish all His purposes for the Jewish people during a period of 70 Weeks of Years (Daniel 9:24), starting with a decree to restore the city of Jerusalem from its destruction by the Babylonians.

The first 483 years of that time period came to an end with the entrance of Jesus into Jerusalem at the beginning of the last week of His life.[1]

Because the Jews rejected Jesus as their Messiah, the clock stopped ticking on Daniel's 70 Weeks of Years (490 years) when Jesus was crucified, and the final 7 years are yet future, as we will see in Part 3 of this book.

Daniel prophesied that after the Messiah was "cut off," the city of Jerusalem and its temple would both suffer another destruction (Daniel 9:26).

Jesus' Confirmation

Jesus Himself confirmed Daniel's prophecy during the last week of His life as He taught His disciples on the Mount of Olives where they sat overlooking the Temple Mount.

He referenced them to the prophecies of Daniel (Matthew 24:15) while pointing at the Temple and saying: "As for these things which you are looking at, the days will come in which there will not be left one stone upon another which will not be torn down" (Luke 21:6).

Later, in the same discourse, Jesus stated that the city would be surrounded by armies which would proceed to desolate it (Luke 21:20). Referring to the Jews in the city at that time, He said, "they will fall by the edge of the sword, and will be led captive into all the nations . . ." (Luke 21:24a).

These prophecies were fulfilled 40 years later in 70 AD when the Romans, under Titus, completely destroyed the city, including the temple — and the Jews were banned from the city.

Gentile Jerusalem

But it should be noted that Jesus made another prophecy about the city in the same speech: He said, "Jerusalem will be trampled under foot by the Gentiles until the times of the Gentiles be fulfilled" (Luke 21:24b). The Romans were followed by the Byzantines, and they were succeeded, in order, by the Muslims, the Crusaders, the Mamelukes, the Turks, the British and the Jordanians.

Just as Jesus prophesied, the city suffered under a long period of Gentile control until June 7, 1967 when — for the first time in 1,897 years — the Jews regained sovereignty over the city. It was on that day that Rabbi Shlomo Goren went to the Western Wall and cried out: "We have taken the City of God. We are entering the Messianic era for the Jewish people."[2]

Another group of prophecies about the city explain why he said these words.

End Time Jerusalem

Four hundred years before Jesus, the prophet Zechariah gave a remarkable series of prophecies about the events that would affect Jerusalem in the end times, right before what we call the Second Coming of the Messiah. These prophecies are recorded in Zechariah 12:1-6. Specifically, the prophecies are as follows:

- The Jews will be back in the land of Israel.
- The Jews will be back in the city of Jerusalem.
- The Israeli army will be like a "firepot among pieces of wood."
- Jerusalem will become the focal point of world politics.
- All the nations of the world will come together against Jerusalem.

Please note that these are prophecies that have been fulfilled! The Jew is back in his land and his city. Despite the minuscule size of the nation, its military forces are considered to be among the most powerful in the world. They have truly been like a "flaming torch among sheaves" in war after war.

Israel became the focal point of world politics in 1973 during the Yom Kippur War. When the West came to the aid of Israel, the Arabs pulled an oil boycott (remember those long gas lines?), bringing the Western nations to their knees. The result was that all the nations of Western Europe withdrew their support from Israel and either took a neutral position or else lined up with the Arabs in their determination to annihilate the Jewish state.[3]

Concerning the last two prophecies cited above, in just the past few years, all the nations of the world, including the United States, have come against Israel, forcing her into a suicidal appeasement policy of trading land for peace. We will discuss this development in detail in the next chapter.

Continuing Controversy

So, the city of Jerusalem is back in the hands of the Jewish people, just as Jesus prophesied it would be (Luke

21:24). But His prophecy has only been partially fulfilled. That's because He indicated that the city would continue to be trampled down by the Gentiles "until the times of the Gentiles be fulfilled." We know from other Scripture passages that the "times of the Gentiles" will not come to an end until the conclusion of the Tribulation and the return of Jesus.

Thus, even today, despite the fact that David Ben-Gurion declared Jerusalem to be Israel's capital on December 5, 1949,[4] the nations of the world have refused to recognize the legitimacy of the declaration and have therefore placed their embassies in Tel Aviv.[5]

In July 1980, the Israeli Knesset passed the "Jerusalem Law" which formally and legally declared Jerusalem the "complete and united" capital of Israel, but the international community continues to denounce this decision.[6]

Further, we also know from prophecies in the book of Revelation that during the Tribulation the city of Jerusalem will once again be conquered by the Gentiles under the leadership of the Antichrist (Revelation 13). The Apostle Paul specifically prophesied about this in 2 Thessalonians 2:1-4 where he stated that during the Tribulation, the Antichrist would enthrone himself in the rebuilt Jewish Temple and would declare himself to be God.

We are commanded in Psalm 122:6 to "pray for the peace of Jerusalem." That peace will not come until the Prince of Peace returns at the end of the Tribulation. Until then, Jerusalem will continue to be oppressed by the Gentile nations of the world.

There are many glorious prophecies concerning Jerusalem during the Millennium and the Eternal State. These will be discussed in chapter 12.

Chapter 11

The Re-focusing of World Politics on Israel

The nation of Israel is, without a doubt, the most hated nation in the world today, and I can prove it quickly and decisively.

Just consider a partial listing of condemnations issued by the United Nations Human Rights Council between 2006, when it was established, and 2015. During that time period, Israel was condemned 61 times, Syria 15 times, North Korea 8 times and Iran 5 times.[1]

Of the 193 members of the United Nations, only 11 nations were condemned, representing six percent. Of the 116 resolutions of condemnation, 53% were aimed at Israel.[2]

Not a one of the following states received a single condemnation despite the fact that all of them have horrible records of human rights violations — Cuba, China, Pakistan, Russia, Saudi Arabia, Egypt, Somalia, and Venezuela.[3]

Yet Israel was condemned 61 times.

Or consider this list of terrorist organizations — ISIS, Al Qaeda, Boko Haram, Fatah, Hamas, Hezbollah and Islamic Jihad. Not a single one of them has been condemned.[4]

Yet Israel was targeted 61 times.

Israel is a democracy that provides the highest standards of freedom for all its citizens, both Jew and Arab.

Yet Israel is condemned.

There is not one Arab country in the world that will allow Jews to be citizens and there is not one that will allow freedom of religion for Jews and Christians.

Yet it is Israel that is condemned.

In contrast, Israel allows Arabs to be citizens and to vote and serve in its parliament. It also provides freedom of speech and religion for both Christians and Muslims.

Yet it is Israel that is condemned.

In the 2015 session of the United Nations Human Rights Council, each of the following nations received one condemnation each — North Korea, Syria and Iran.[5]

Israel received 4!

That means that 98% of the 193 member states of the United Nations — inhabited by 6.6 billion people — have gotten no mention at all in the resolutions of the UN Human Rights Council.

Further, the resolutions of the United Nations are often the height of silliness. For example, in 2016 the UN Commission on the Status of Women passed a resolution blaming Israel for the fact that a public opinion poll showed that 51% of the women living in the Gaza Strip had been beaten by their husbands![6]

The beating of wives is a known cultural phenomenon of Islam and is even approved in the Qur'an (Sura 4:34 and 38: 44), yet Israel is blamed for it!

Israel is one of the smallest nations in the world. It is only 263 miles long and 71 miles wide — about the size of the state of New Jersey. Does the United Nations really believe it is the source of all the world's problems?

Anti-Semitism in Europe

Further evidence of the world's hatred of the Jewish people is to be found in the rising wave of anti-Semitism that is currently sweeping Europe and the emigration to Israel that it is provoking. It is a phenomenon that was featured on the cover of *Newsweek* magazine in August of 2014.[7]

Here's how a feature article in *US News and World Report* put it in April of 2015:[8]

> Seventy years after the Holocaust, anti-Semitism is again growing more virulent in Europe. From Toulouse to Paris, London to Berlin, Brussels to Copenhagen, Jews are being harassed, assaulted and even killed.

According to the Pew Research Center, by 2013, Jews were being harassed in 34 of 45 European countries and anti-Semitic harassment worldwide had reached a seven-year high.[9]

All over Europe, and particularly in Greece, France and Belgium, Jews are seeing their religious freedoms violated, their cemeteries vandalized, and their synagogues desecrated. They are also experiencing increasing personal attacks that often result in death.

In France, the annual number of anti-Semitic incidents is currently seven times as high as in the 1990s. In 2014, they doubled.[10]

The elections to the European Parliament in 2014 showed a surge of support for extreme right-wing Neo-Nazi parties in France, Greece, Hungary and Germany.[11]

The population of Europe today is 742 million. Only 1.4 million of those are Jews.[12] That means the Jews constitute only 0.2% of the population, and yet they are the focus of hatred and persecution. And in the process, they are blamed for most of Europe's problems.

Anti-Semitism Among Evangelicals

Perhaps one of the most disturbing trends today that clearly shows the deep-rooted nature of Jewish hatred is the rapidly growing anti-Zionist attitude within Christendom, and, yes, even among Evangelicals.

Consider this Internet headline: "Hanegraaff and Burge Attack Christian Support of Israel."[13] Gary Burge is a theology professor at Wheaton College, an Evangelical school. Hank Hanegraaff is the host of the *Bible Answer Man* radio program that is broadcast nationwide. Both are vehement "Anti-Zionists."

And in that regard, let me repeat a very important point that I made earlier in chapter 2: anti-Zionism is just anti-Semitism in new, sophisticated clothes. Whereas anti-Semitism sought to drive out the Jews from the lands where they lived, anti-Zionism refuses to accept their right to live in their own land.

In addition to falsely claiming that the Jews stole the land of Israel from the Palestinians, more and more Evangelical spokesmen are arguing that the land promises that were made to the Jews in the Old Testament were fulfilled under Joshua.

Really? Pictured on the next page is the land promised to the descendants of Abraham. The Jews have never come close to occupying it.

Despite these statements, when the anti-Zionists are accused of being anti-Semitic, they deny the accusation vehemently. Here's how Dennis Prager, radio host and political commentator, has replied to their denials in his book, *Why the Jews?*:[14]

> The contention that anti-Zionists are not enemies of Jews, despite the advocacy of

> policies that would lead to the mass murder of Jews, is, to put it as generously as possible, disingenuous.
>
> If anti-Zionism realized its goal, another Jewish holocaust would take place . . . Therefore attempts to draw distinctions between anti-Zionism and anti-Semitism are simply meant to fool the naive.

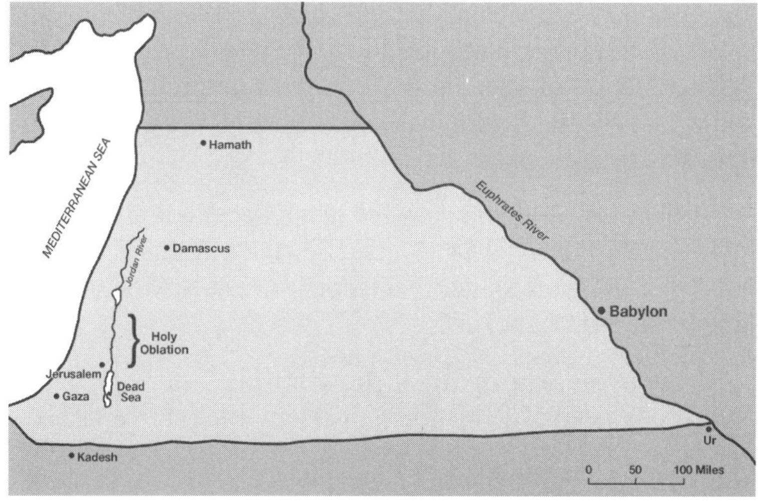

The Abrahamic Land Promise

Christian Palestinianism

In recent years a new form of this anti-Zionism has raised its ugly head in the form of the Christian Palestinian Movement.

James Showers, Director of The Friends of Israel, has defined the movement in the following words:[15]

> Christian Palestinianism claims modern Israel has no biblical connection with or justification for owning the Promised Land; therefore, it concludes, Israel has become an apartheid state, occupying territory belonging

to the Palestinian Arabs.

The Movement's most prominent leaders over the past few years are the following:

Stephen Sizer — Anglican vicar of Christ Church in Surrey, England. He is a vicious anti-Semite who has led the Christian Palestinian Movement until recently. He has denounced Israel as an "apartheid state" which he claims is guilty of ethnic cleansing.[16]

Further, he has demonized Christians who support Israel as "heretical Armageddonites" whose interpretation of the Bible "provides a theological endorsement for racial segregation, apartheid and war."[17]

In January of 2016 he posted to his Facebook page a link to an article titled, "9/11 — Israel did it." The article theorized that the Israeli intelligence organization, Mossad, was behind the 9/11 attacks.[18]

That action was the final straw for his superior, Bishop Andrew Watson. The bishop issued a public rebuke of Sizer and demanded that he stop speaking and writing about Israel, or else lose his ministry as a parish priest. Sizer agreed.[19]

Gary Burge — Ordained Presbyterian minister and professor of New Testament at Wheaton College in Illinois. He is the American leader of the movement and will most likely succeed Sizer as the international leader.

Donald E. Wagner — Ordained Presbyterian minister and director of the Center for Middle Eastern Studies at North Park University in Chicago, Illinois.

John Stott — The late theologian and rector emeritus of All Souls Church in London.

Hank Hanegraaff — President of the Christian Research Institute and host of the *Bible Answer Man* radio program.

Tony Campolo — Baptist minister, author, and professor emeritus of sociology at Eastern University in Pennsylvania.

Lynne Hybels — Wife of Willow Creek Church senior pastor and founder, Bill Hybels.

One of the movement's greatest propaganda tools is the Kairos Palestine Document adopted in 2009. It declares "that the Israeli occupation of Palestinian land is a sin against God and humanity . . ." And it further asserts that:[20]

> Any theology, seemingly based on the Bible or on faith or on history, that legitimizes the occupation, is far from Christian teachings, because it calls for violence and holy war in the name of God Almighty . . .

That's a mouthful when you consider the fact that it is Muslims, not Christians and Jews, who are calling for Holy War in the name of God.

The proponents of the movement hold Christian Zionists in open contempt. Before his death, John Stott, the renowned British Evangelical leader, denounced Christian Zionism as "biblically anathema to the Christian faith."[21]

Hank Hanegraaff wrote, "Christian Zionist beliefs and behaviors are the antithesis of biblical Christianity."[22]

One British journalist, Alan Hart, who supports the Christian Palestinian Movement, went so far as to state on his website:[23]

> It's time to give Israel's hardcore Zionists their real name. They are the New Nazis . . . If Europeans and Americans don't stop the New Nazis, it's likely their endgame will be the extermination of millions of Palestinians.

The Sources of Jewish Hatred

This brings us to our crucial question: Why is there such universal hatred of the Jews and the nation of Israel?

ISLAM — Let's begin with Islam. The Muslim world hates the Jews because it is commanded to do so in their holy book, *The Qur'an*.

When Mohammad began dictating the Qur'an over a period of 23 years, his initial statements about both Jews and Christians were very positive because he expected them to embrace his new religion. He called them "the people of the Book" (Sura 3:199). Here is one of the Qur'an's favorable verses regarding Christians and Jews (Sura 5:69):

> Those who believe [in the Qur'an], those who follow the Jewish [Scriptures], and the Christians and the Sabians — any who believe in God and the Last Day, and work righteousness, on them shall be no fear, nor shall they grieve.

But when Christians and Jews refused to accept Islam, Mohammad received new revelations that demeaned them and ordered them to be killed if they did not submit. For example here are three of his later revelations:

1) A command to not take Jews and Christians as friends (Sura 5:51).

2) A command to fight against Jews and Christians until they either submit to Allah or agree to pay a special tax (Hadith: *Sahih Muslim* 19:4294).

3) A reference to Jews as "apes and swine to be despised and rejected" (Sura 2:65-66 and 5:60)

You must keep in mind that Islam is totally intolerant of any other religion. The very word, Islam, means "submission." In fact, the Qur'an commands intolerance toward all other religions:

> Take not Jews and Christians for friends . . . He among you who takes them for friends is one of them . . . Choose not for friends such of those who received the Scripture before you [Jews and Christians] . . . But keep your duty to Allah (Sura 5:51,55,57).
>
> [For those who do not submit to Allah] their punishment is . . . execution or crucifixion, or the cutting off of hands and feet, from the opposite sides, or exile from the land (Sura 5:33).

The Qur'an also expresses an intolerant attitude toward any Muslim who decides to reject the Islamic faith or convert to another religion.

> Sura 9:12 commands that apostates are to be executed.
>
> Hadith 9:57 says "Whoever changes his religion, kill him."

These commands are practiced in all Islamic Fundamentalist countries today. There is absolutely no religious freedom in any nation of the world that is ruled by Muslims.

Keep in mind also that complete conquest of the world is the goal of Islam. Here's how the Qur'an puts it (Sura 2:190-193):

> Fight in the way of Allah . . . and slay them [the unbelievers] wherever you find them and drive them out . . . and fight them until . . . their religion is for Allah.

In like manner, Muslims are commanded (Sura 2:193 & 8:39):

> To fight non-Muslims until you exterminate all other religions, leaving Islam as the one and only religion in the world.

Muslims in Western non-Muslim countries try to discount these commands by quoting verses from the Qur'an that sound very tolerant:

> There is no compulsion in religion (Sura 2:256).

> You will find that those who are nearest in love to the believers [Muslims] are those who say, "We are Christians" (Sura 5:82).

Yes, these verses sound wonderful, but what the defenders of Islam do not tell you is that there is a rule for interpreting the Qur'an, called the "Rule of Abrogation," that says that later revelations to Muhammad overrule earlier revelations, if there is a conflict.[24]

They have to have this rule because there are a lot of contradictions in the Qur'an. In fact, there are 193 verses in the Qur'an that have been abrogated by later verses, and all verses that speak kindly of Christians and Jews have been abrogated.[25]

CHRISTIANITY— Let's turn our attention now to Christian anti-Semitism.

Whereas Muslim hatred of the Jews dates back 1,400 years to the founding of Islam, Christian hatred dates back 1,900 years to within 100 years of the establishment of the Church.

The irony, of course is that the Church was founded by Jews and was 100 percent Jewish until the conversion of the Roman solider Cornelius. But within 100 years of the

Church's birth, Gentiles were dominating its membership, and Jews were being pushed aside and scorned as "Christ Killers."

The record of Christian anti-Semitism is a very sordid one which I detailed in chapter 2. As that chapter clearly and tragically demonstrates, most of the anti-Semitism in the world throughout the centuries has originated with Christians who were taught by the Roman Catholic Church that Jews were to be despised because they were guilty of killing God.

This hatred became codified in Church documents, and it became manifest in Replacement Theology and systematic persecution of the Jews. They were slaughtered in the Crusades, they were parodied in the Passion Plays, they were blamed for the Black Plague, they were required to wear distinguishing marks and they were herded into ghettos.

Martin Luther came to despise the Jews because they refused to accept his reformed Gospel based on faith and grace rather than works. By the end of his life, Luther had turned against the Jews with a vengeance. In 1543 he wrote a pamphlet entitled "Concerning the Jews and Their Lies."[26] In it he laid out a blueprint for dealing with them that Hitler endorsed and which laid the foundation for the Holocaust.

This is the reason that the Jewish people view the Holocaust as a Christian inspired event, and rightfully so, for it was the natural outcome of 1,900 years of Christian hatred.

WORLDWIDE — We have seen why Christians and Muslims hate Jews and Israel, but what is fascinating and even chilling is that worldwide there are people who are neither Christians nor Muslims who hate the Jews — many of which have never even met a Jew!

For example, ever since the early 1980's a whole series of books have been published in Japan that blame the Jews for many of Japan's problems and argue that the whole world suffers from an international Jewish conspiracy.[27]

How is all this hatred of the Jews to be explained?

I would argue that all forms of anti-Semitism have the same root, which is Satan himself. You see, I believe that anti-Semitism is supernaturally inspired by Satan. That's because Satan hates the Jews with a passion for several reasons:

1) God chose them to be His witness to the world.

2) Through them God gave the world the Bible.

3) Through them God gave the world the Messiah.

4) God has promised that He will save a great remnant of them.

5) God has promised that through that remnant He will bless all the nations of the world during the Millennial reign of Jesus.

Satan is determined to destroy every Jew on planet Earth so that God cannot keep His promises to them.

That's what the Holocaust was all about.

And, as we will see in section 3 of this book, during the last half of the Tribulation, Satan is going to try once more to destroy the Jews by inspiring the Antichrist to annihilate them.

America's Relationship

Ever since the re-establishment of the state of Israel in May of 1948, the United States has been the nation's best ally and strongest supporter.

That does not mean that there have been no tensions. Even though **President Truman** was the first to recognize the existence of the Jewish state,[28] he immediately slapped an arms embargo on Israel in the naive hope it would prevent violence in the Middle East.[29]

President Eisenhower always supported Israel in words, but behind the scenes, he applied great pressure for Israel to withdraw from the Sinai Peninsula after the Suez War ended in 1956.[30] In fact, he became the first president to threaten Israel when the Israelis dragged their feet about withdrawing. He told them either to withdraw or else he would withhold more than $100 million in U.S. aid. He also supported a UN resolution condemning Israel for not withdrawing,[31] and he also continued the arms embargo.

President Kennedy was a strong supporter of Israel in both word and deed. He called Israel "the child of hope and the home of the brave."[32] He added: "Israel carries the shield of democracy and it honors the sword of freedom."[33]

Kennedy lifted the arms embargo and extended the first informal security guarantees to Israel in 1962. And beginning in 1963, he authorized the sale to Israel of advanced U.S. weaponry, including surface-to-air Hawk missiles.[34]

President Johnson quickly emerged as one of the greatest friends of Israel among modern day presidents. During his administration, the U.S. became Israel's chief diplomatic ally and primary arms supplier.

Johnson strongly supported Israel during the 1967 Six Day War, approving the sale of tanks and fighter jets.[35] He also closely supervised the crafting of UN Resolution 242 in 1967 which called for Israel to be guaranteed "secure and recognized boundaries."[36]

President Nixon is considered today to have been anti-Semitic, based upon ugly statements he made about the Jews that are contained on the infamous White House tapes.

But when it came to Israel, he was a realist in foreign policy who recognized the importance of the only democratic state in the Middle East.

Thus, when Israel suffered a surprise invasion in the 1973 Yom Kippur War, Nixon responded immediately with overwhelming aid to counter the offensive. He did so despite the fact that he knew it would alienate the Arab World and greatly endanger our relationship with the Soviet Union.[37]

During his short three year tenure in the presidency (1974-77), **President Ford** took a hard line stance toward Israel, demanding that they withdraw from the Sinai which they had re-conquered during the Yom Kippur War.[38] When the Israelis continued to stall in response to his demands, Ford put the brakes on an Israeli request for F-15 fighter planes and froze all scheduled deliveries of arms.[39]

President Carter put the Sinai issue on the front burner when he assumed the presidency, and in 1979 he was able to broker a deal between Israel and Egypt which provided for peace between the two nations and a complete withdrawal of Israel from the Sinai Peninsula.[40] Unfortunately, in recent years, Carter's writings have revealed that he is a vehement anti-Semite who detests the Israelis.[41]

President Reagan has the reputation of being the most pro-Israel president in American history. Much of that reputation is based on glowing words that he often spoke in support of Israel.[42]

But Reagan had a number of run-ins with Israel.[43] For example, in 1981 he significantly strengthened the Arabs by selling them some of our most sophisticated weapons. He did this despite great opposition by both the Israelis and the Israeli lobby in the Congress.[44] And when the Israelis bombed the Iraqi nuclear reactor in 1981, Reagan supported the UN Security Council resolution that condemned Israel.[45]

On the other hand, in 1985 Reagan began to provide Israel with $3 billion in foreign aid annually, all in the form of grants.[46]

When Israel launched the war in Lebanon in 1982 to clear the PLO out of the country, Reagan initially supported it, but he soon soured on the operation. He pressured the Israelis to end it, and he helped arrange for Arafat and the PLO leadership to escape into exile in Tunisia.[47]

More significantly, in 1988 Reagan authorized the State Department to enter into dialogue with the PLO, reversing the U.S. policy of refusing to recognize terrorist organizations.[48]

The First Bush Presidency proved to be ***the decisive turning point*** in U.S.-Israel relations. **George H. W. Bush** came to power in 1989, and he had hardly assumed office before his anti-Semitic Secretary of State, James Baker, proclaimed that the time had come for Israel to "abandon its expansionist policies."[49] Which made Israel supporters wonder what he was talking about!

Bush added fuel to the fire when he announced in 1991 that he considered East Jerusalem to be "occupied territory," despite the fact that Israel had officially annexed it in 1980.[50]

Following the Gulf War in 1991, President Bush decided to pursue an Arab-Israeli settlement by convening an international conference in Madrid, Spain. He forced the Israelis to attend by making their participation a condition for the U.S. to provide $10 billion in loan guarantees to the World Bank. Israel needed the money to deal with an overwhelming influx of immigrants from the Soviet Union.[51]

The Madrid Conference laid the groundwork for ***the Oslo Accords in 1993 which initiated the Land-for-Peace process*** whereby Israel would surrender land in exchange for promises of peace.[52]

President Clinton tried to position himself as a strong friend of Israel. He provided the nation with substantial financial aid, but he worked constantly behind the scenes to convince Israel to trade land-for-peace.

He presided over the signing of the Oslo Accords at the White House in September of 1993.[53] It was these agreements that implemented the land-for-peace concept, starting with the Israeli withdrawal from Jericho.

In 1998 Clinton hosted the Wye River Conference between Arafat and Netanyahu which resulted in Israel agreeing to withdraw from the ancient Jewish city of Hebron.[54] And in 2000, Clinton convened the Camp David Conference between Arafat and Israeli Prime Minister Ehud Barak — the most liberal prime minister in Israel's history.

Barak agreed to give Arafat all that he had ever demanded in diplomatic circles, and to the astonishment of all present, Arafat responded by getting up and walking out of the room. He immediately flew back to Israel and launched the Second Intifada.[55]

Arafat's action made it clear he had no interest in peace with Israel and would never be satisfied with the establishment of a second Palestinian state. His clear goal instead was the annihilation of Israel.

President George W. Bush came to power by confirming to Israel's Prime Minister, Ariel Sharon, that he was not going to follow his father's hard-line policy toward Israel.[56] But hardly had he given this assurance, when in 2001 he turned around and ***called for the establishment of a Palestinian State***, the first American president to do so publicly and formally, proceeding to make it an official part of U.S. foreign policy.[57]

Bush also picked up on the Land-for-Peace strategy by demanding that Israel surrender the Gaza Strip. And in the midst of the painful withdrawal in the summer of 2005, Bush's Secretary of State, Condoleezza Rice, proclaimed: "Everyone empathizes with what the Israelis are doing, but it cannot be Gaza only."[58]

President Obama emerged quickly as the most anti-Israel president in U.S. history. His very first television interview was granted shortly after his inauguration to the Muslim network, Al Arabiya.[59] He followed this up by dashing off to Cairo, Egypt in June of 2009 to give his infamous apology speech to the Muslim nations of the Middle East.[60]

In that speech he started developing one of his major lines of thought concerning Israel — namely, that the experience of the Jews in the Holocaust is the moral equivalent of what the Palestinians are experiencing under Israeli "occupation."

A month later, in July 2009, Obama announced that the time had come for "daylight" between the United States and Israel.[61] In March of 2010, Obama met with Prime Minister Netanyahu at the White House. The Israeli prime minister was ushered in a side door like a secret mistress and treated with disdain like the dictator of a banana republic. No press or photos were allowed.[62]

Obama demanded Israel's withdrawal from Jewish settlements, and when Netanyahu balked, the president said it was time for him to eat dinner with his family — at which point he walked out and left the prime minister and his aides alone, offering them no food or drink.[63]

In May of 2011 the president went on national TV to demand that Israel return to the suicidal borders that existed before the Six Day War in 1967.[64] Three years later, in 2014, a spokesperson for the State Department, Jen Psaki, announced that the Obama Administration ***no longer considered it necessary for the Palestinians to recognize the existence of the State of Israel!***[65]

Throughout his administration, Obama continued to condemn Israel's settlements as being "illegitimate,"[66] he continued to provide the Palestinian Authority with over $600 million in aid each year,[67] and before leaving office, he lifted the United States veto in the Security Council in order to allow the Council to pass a resolution denouncing Israel's settlements and declaring East Jerusalem, including the Temple Mount, to belong to the Palestinians.[68]

Our nation's double-cross of our most important ally was complete.

Summary

As you can see, the record of U.S. relations with Israel has been erratic from the start.

Even President Truman, who offered immediate recognition, decided to slap an arms embargo on the fledgling nation.

Since that time, we have often treated the Jewish nation with disdain, forcing its leaders to do whatever we desired through the manipulation of foreign aid and through threats of one kind or another.

And, the Israeli government has had little choice but to conform to our demands. That's because the stark reality is that our veto in the UN Security Council is the only thing that prevents the world from placing draconian sanctions on Israel that would destroy the nation's economy in short order.

Overall, I would say that until Obama, the Democrat Presidents have been much more favorable to Israel than have the Republicans.

In recent years, since the early 1990s, we have become increasingly hostile to Israel as we have literally forced them to take the self-defeating path of appeasement. Additionally, year after year, we have insulted the people of Israel by refusing to recognize Jerusalem as their capital.

Think for a moment about what an incredible insult this is to the Jewish people. It is equivalent to the Israelis declaring that they do not recognize Washington, DC as our capital, and then proceeding to place their Embassy in Chicago.

Yet, despite our checkered record of support, we have been Israel's best friend. They have been the largest cumulative recipient of U.S. foreign assistance since World War II. To date, the United States has provided Israel with $121 billion in aid, almost all of it in the form of military assistance.[69]

The Future

But the handwriting is on the wall. The days of American support are numbered. The time has come for the Israeli leadership to face up to the fact that its hope and trust needs to be placed in Almighty God and not in the United States.

In like manner, the time has come for our nation to realize that in our manhandling of Israel, we are courting the wrath of God.

President Donald Trump assumed office with a promise to move the American Embassy to Jerusalem and to support the right of Israel to establish settlements in the Palestinian area.[70] However, hardly had he taken the oath of office when he began to backpedal on his promise to move the Embassy,[71] and he suddenly declared that he had decided that the Jewish settlements are an impediment to peace.[72] He also announced that he was going to assign his son-in-law, Jared Kushner, to negotiate a peace settlement between Israel and the Palestinians.[73]

Since the problems in the Middle East are spiritual in nature and not political ones, Trump is going to discover that the place is a political quagmire, and when he runs into a stone wall, he is likely to become impatient with the Israelis and start putting impossible pressures on them once again.

According to end time prophecies, Israel is not going to experience peace until it is negotiated and enforced by the Antichrist. And even then, it will be a peace that will endure for only three years. True peace will not come to Israel until the Prince of Peace returns.

Obama's Last Gasp

In mid-January of 2017, right before Donald Trump was sworn in as President, Obama not only stopped protecting Israel from the United Nations by lifting our veto, he also endorsed an international conference held in Paris, France which was attended by the representatives of 70 nations, including the United States. The conference was held for the purpose of applying pressure to Israel to accept a "two-state solution."[74]

Although the conference proved to be "the mouse that roared," because its resolutions had no binding power in international law, it was, nonetheless, a very significant gathering in view of the fact that Bible prophecy states that all the nations of the world will come together against Israel in the end times (Zechariah 12:3).

A Doomed Policy

The land-for-peace appeasement policy that we have forced upon Israel is certain to fail. History proves conclusively that a policy of appeasement never works because all it does is whet the appetite of the aggressor. Winston Churchill put it this way: "An appeaser is one who feeds a crocodile, hoping it will eat him last."[75]

Both the world's political leaders and the Humanistic leaders of Israel are deceived into believing that the Arab-Israeli crisis is a political one that can be solved with political compromise. But the fact of the matter is that it is not a political crisis — it is a spiritual one that is immune to political settlement.

Biblical Warnings

The Bible says that whoever touches the Jewish people, touches the "apple of God's eye" (Zechariah 2:8). The Bible also says in Psalm 129 that no blessing should ever be bestowed on any anti-Semite. Here's how the passage reads:

> 5) May all who hate Zion be put to shame and turned backward.
>
> 6) Let them be like grass upon the housetops, which withers before it grows up,
>
> 7) With which the reaper does not fill his hand, or the binder of sheaves, his bosom.
>
> 8) Nor do those who pass by say, "The blessing of the LORD be upon you; we bless you in the name of the LORD!"

These are ominous words for those who hate the Jewish people and the nation of Israel.

People object by saying, "But the Jewish people do not deserve our respect or God's love. They are a rebellious, stiff-necked people who deserve condemnation."

My response to that statement is this: "Do you deserve God's love?" Of course not! None of us do.

God's Lovingkindness

God's continuing love for the Jewish people in the midst of their persistent rebellion is a demonstration of God's grace. They were originally called to be God's Chosen People — to serve as witnesses of what it means to have a relationship with the true God of this universe.

And they continue in that capacity today, even while they are still in a state of rebellion and are thus under the discipline of God. Their history clearly shows that when you are faithful to God, He blesses; when you are unfaithful, He disciplines; and when you repent, He forgives, forgets, and starts blessing again.

What grace! What glorious grace!

Here's how the Apostle Paul put it (Romans 11:33):

> Oh, the depth of the riches both of the wisdom and knowledge of God! How unsearchable are His judgments and unfathomable His ways!

Part 3

The Future

Chapter 12

The Redemption of Israel

We now come to the Bible prophecies concerning the Jewish people in the future — prophecies yet to be fulfilled. And there are many.

They begin with incredibly bad news for Israel, but they conclude with glorious news that far outweighs the bad. The prophesied future of the Jewish people could be summed up in two words: wrath and glory.

The wrath relates to a terrible seven year period of unparalleled suffering which the Hebrew Scriptures refer to as "the time of Jacob's distress" (Jeremiah 30:7). This period is usually referred to in Christian writings as "The Tribulation."

The coming glory relates to the salvation of a great Jewish remnant and their elevation to the status of the primary nation in the world.

I. Warfare and Triumph

The first unfulfilled prophecies related to Israel concern warfare — something that is not new to the Jewish people. Ever since the re-establishment of their nation in 1948, the Jews of Israel have been in almost a constant state of war. Consider:

The War of Independence	1948-1949
The Suez War	1956
The Six Day War	1967
The War of Attrition	1967-1970

The Yom Kippur War	1973
The First Lebanon War	1982
The First Intifada (Arab Uprising)	1987-1993
The Second Intifada	2000-2005
The Second Lebanon War	2006
The First Gaza War	2008-2009
The Second Gaza War	2012
The Third Gaza War	2014

This perpetual state of war is in accordance with a prophecy by Isaiah which stated that the birth pangs of the re-establishment of the state of Israel in the end times would come *after* the birth of the state (Isaiah 66:7-8).

So, what about the future?

The Scriptures indicate that there are two major wars waiting on the horizon for the Jewish people. The first is a war with an inner ring of Arab states that have a common border with Israel. The second will be against a coalition of Muslim nations in an outer ring around Israel. This second war will be led by Russia.

The Psalm 83 War

The first of these wars — the one against the inner ring of Arab states, is described in Psalm 83. It is portrayed as a war to "wipe out" the Jewish people "as a nation" (Psalm 83:4). The specific coalition that is mentioned in this psalm is composed of Lebanon, Syria, Jordan, Egypt and Gaza — all the states that have a common border with Israel.

Some prophecy experts discount Psalm 83 as a future war. They argue the psalm is not a prophecy, but is just a lament. But it was written by Asaph who was a prophet (2 Chronicles 29:30), and Bill Salus, in his book, *Isralestine*, makes a strong argument in behalf of the fact that the passage is an unfulfilled prophecy.[1]

Psalm 83 does not tell how the war turns out, but we know from other passages that Israel will win all of its end time wars. For example, Zechariah 12:6, speaking of the end times, says: "In that day I will make the clans of Judah like a firepot among pieces of wood and a flaming torch among sheaves, so they will consume on the right hand and on the left all the surrounding peoples, while the inhabitants of Jerusalem again dwell on their own sites in Jerusalem."

Zechariah continues in verse 8 to say that in the end times Israel will be like David against Goliath and "the house of David will be like God, like the angel of the LORD . . ." And that has certainly been the case in all the wars Israel has fought since the establishment of the state.

And what a miracle this has been! Just think about the fact that Israel has a Jewish population of only 6.5 million Jews, and they are surrounded by over 350 million Arabs who desire to destroy them. Yet, Israel has emerged victorious in every war. Such military power, and the effective use of it, has to be miraculous.

So, there seems to be no doubt that the Israeli Defense Forces (IDF) will prove successful in the Psalm 83 War, bringing peace and stability to Israel. But such a victory will undoubtedly cause the remaining Muslim nations of the Middle East to panic and reach out to their natural ally — Russia.

And, of course, the Russians will respond to the Muslim call for help with overwhelming enthusiasm because they have long desired an excuse for invading the Middle East and gaining control of that region's abundant oil and gas reserves.

The War of Ezekiel 38 & 39

The Russian response brings us to the second prophesied war — the War of Gog and Magog that is described in detail in Ezekiel 38 and 39. Russia is depicted as invading Israel with a coalition of states that today are all Muslim. Further, these states constitute an outer ring around Israel. The Russian allies include Iran (and possibly Iraq), Ethiopia (including the Sudan), Libya (and possibly Algeria), and Turkey (Ezekiel 38:1-6). The likelihood that the Psalm 83 War will precede this conflict is reflected in the fact that none of the nations having a common border with Israel are included in the Russian coalition.

Another factor that indicates the Gog and Magog War will come after the Psalm 83 War is that Ezekiel's prophecy says the Russian invasion will take place at a time when Israel is living "securely" and "without walls" (Ezekiel 38:11,14). That certainly is not the current situation. Israel exists today in a sea of insecurity, and it has a security wall that meanders down the center of the nation for nearly 400 miles.

Except for these preconditions, the timing of the War of Gog and Magog is a mystery. The consensus of opinion for many years has been that the war would start at the beginning of the Tribulation, after the Antichrist has signed a treaty guaranteeing the peace of Israel.

But in recent years some strong arguments have been presented for the war to start before the beginning of the Tribulation. Ron Rhodes, in his book, *Northern Storm Rising,* presents a very convincing argument for the Gog and Magog War starting at least 3½ years before the Tribulation.[2]

One of his arguments is that Ezekiel 39:9 says that when the war is over, the Jews will "make fires with the weapons and burn them . . . for seven years." This is most likely a reference to all the fuel that will be captured. In the past, commentators have tended to identify these seven years with the seven year length of the Tribulation. But this cannot be because, as Rhodes points out, the Jews are going to be driven out of their homeland by the Antichrist in the middle of the Tribulation (Revelation 12:13-17). This means the Jews are going to be in the land only during the first 3½ years of the Tribulation. 

But regardless of its timing, the War of Gog and Magog is going to have a profound spiritual impact on Israel. God Almighty Himself — and not the IDF — is going to supernaturally destroy the invading armies with earthquakes, pestilence, torrential rains, fire and brimstone, and battlefield confusion (Ezekiel 38;19-22 and Ezekiel 39:4-6).

When the Jewish people witness their supernatural deliverance from certain destruction, many will turn their hearts to God. The Lord says that on the day of victory, He will set His glory among the nations (Ezekiel 39:21), "and the house of Israel will know I am the LORD their God from that day onward" (Ezekiel 39:22).

II. Tribulation and Survival

With Israel's victories in these two wars, the nation will truly be living in peace and security when the Tribulation begins.

From a Jewish viewpoint, the Tribulation should be called "Daniel's 70th Week of Years." This terminology refers to the fact that Daniel prophesied a period of 70 weeks of years (490 years) during which six goals would be accomplished among the Jewish people. The goals were (Daniel 9:24):

1) "To finish the transgression" (by accepting the Messiah).

2) "To make an end of sin" (the repentance of a remnant).

3) "To make atonement for iniquity" (the Messiah to die for sins).

4) "To bring in everlasting righteousness" (the establishment of the Messiah's millennial reign).

5) "To seal up vision and prophecy" (fulfill all Messianic prophecies).

6) "To anoint the most holy place" (begin the construction of the Millennial Temple).

As you can see, only one of these aims has been fulfilled — the Messiah's atonement for sin. All the rest remain unfulfilled. Four hundred eighty-three years of Daniel's prophecy led up to the crucifixion of Jesus (Daniel 9:26). The last seven years remain, during which all the rest of God's aims for the Jewish people will be met.

A Prophetic Gap

The Angel Gabriel indicated to Daniel that there would be a prophetic gap between the first 483 years of the prophecy and the last seven years (Daniel 9:27). He did this by stating that the 70th week of the prophecy (the last seven years) would not begin until the Antichrist appears on the scene and makes a 'firm covenant" with Israel (Daniel 9:27).

It's similar to the timing of a football game. All such games are scheduled to last four quarters of 15 minutes each, or a total of one hour. But most games run three hours or more, depending on the number of time-outs and the length of the half-time break. Thus, at the death of the Messiah, God called a "time-out" on the 70 weeks of years in order to discipline the Jewish people for rejecting their Messiah. We are now waiting for the Antichrist treaty, which will signal the start of the last seven years.

No one knows for sure what will be the nature of that treaty. Most believe it will be some sort of peace treaty the Antichrist will negotiate between Israel and the surrounding Arab states which will allow Israel to rebuild its Temple. This assumption is based on the fact that Bible prophecies make it clear that Israel will rebuild its Third Temple and will have it completed by the middle of the seven year period of the Tribulation (2 Thessalonians 2:1-4 and Revelation 11:1-2).

The Antichrist

Some teach that the Jewish people will be so overcome with the political work in their behalf by the Antichrist, that they will receive him as their Messiah. This is based on a statement of Jesus when He said, "I have come in My Father's name, and you do not receive Me; if another comes in his own name, you will receive him" (John 5:43).

It is true that the Jewish people will receive the Antichrist as a political savior, but the Scriptures make it clear that they will never accept him as their Messiah. We know that because the book of Revelation reveals that when the Antichrist enters the rebuilt Temple in the middle of the Tribulation and declares himself to be God, the Jewish people will immediately reject him, and he will turn on them with a vengeance, determined to annihilate them (Revelation 12:13-17).

The 144,000

When the Tribulation begins, the Scriptures tell us that the Jewish people will play a very important role during that seven year period. For one thing, the supernatural victory of Israel in the War of Gog and Magog will turn the hearts of many Jews to God and their Messiah, Yeshua, and 144,000 of them will be sealed by the Holy Spirit for redemption (Revelation 7:1-8). They are referred to as "bond servants of our God" (Revelation 7:3), and that certainly must mean they will be evangelists who will commit themselves to the proclamation of the Gospel.

We are told that they will be supernaturally protected by God throughout the seven years of the Tribulation, and they are pictured standing in triumph with Jesus on Mount Zion in Jerusalem when He returns at the end of the Tribulation

(Revelation 14:1-5).

The Two Witnesses

Two other key players during the Tribulation are Two Witnesses of God who will appear in Jerusalem and will daily preach the Gospel and call the world to repentance. Like the 144,000, these two men will be supernaturally protected until the middle of the Tribulation when their protection will be lifted, and the Antichrist will kill them.

These two men are not identified. Many of the early Church Fathers thought they would be Enoch and Elijah. Most prophecy experts today think they will be Moses and Elijah, based on the miracles they perform.

I believe one of them will definitely be Elijah, for we are told in Malachi 4:5 that Elijah will return to this earth before "the great and terrible day of the LORD" (Malachi 4:5). I also believe the other man will be Enoch. Like Elijah, he was taken to Heaven before he experienced death. Unlike Elijah, he was a Gentile. Thus, with Enoch and Elijah, the world would have two prophetic voices during the first half of the Tribulation — one speaking to the Jews and the other to the Gentiles.

Peace for Israel but Carnage for the World

The first half of the Tribulation is going to be a time of peace for the nation of Israel while the rest of the world is engulfed in war. Although the Antichrist will rise to power in Europe through his brilliance and cunning (Daniel 8:23-26), he is not going to be received with joy by Africa, Asia and Latin America — all of which have spent the last 200 years throwing off European colonialism. And when the Antichrist establishes his One World Religion, you can be assured that the Muslim world will reject him.

Thus, the Antichrist is going to have to use military power to conquer the world. Revelation chapter 6 describes the beginning of that war, resulting in one-fourth of the world's population being killed. Then, in Revelation 8 and 9 it appears that the Antichrist's war of conquest morphs into a nuclear war, resulting in the slaughter of one-third of those who are left.

If the Lord takes out approximately one billion people in the Rapture of the Church before the Tribulation begins, that would leave six billion souls here on the earth. One-fourth of them would be 1.5 billion people, leaving a population of 4.5 billion. One-third of those remaining would be another 1.5 billion. So, by the middle of the Tribulation, one half of the population of the earth — three billion — will be dead.

III. Repentance & Salvation

During the talk Jesus made to His disciples on the Mount of Olives during the last week of His life, He referred to the second half of the Tribulation as the "great tribulation." (Matthew 24:21). This has motivated many prophecy scholars to proclaim that the first half of the Tribulation will be relatively peaceful, but nothing could be further from the truth. How could the second half of the Tribulation be worse when one half of the world's population is going to die in the first half?

Keep in mind that Jesus was talking to a Jewish audience. His point was that for the Jewish people, the last half of the Tribulation would be the "great tribulation."

The "Great Tribulation" for the Jews

And that is precisely what the Scriptures teach. We are told in 2 Thessalonians 2:1-4 that the Antichrist will enter the rebuilt Jewish Temple in Jerusalem and declare himself to be God, and when the Jews reject him as their Messiah, he will turn against them with a vengeance and will try to annihilate them (Revelation 12:13-17). He will slaughter them right and left as they flee their homeland to a special place of protection that God has prepared for them in the modern day nation of Jordan (Daniel 11:41).

The prophet Zechariah says that the slaughter worldwide will be so great that two-thirds of the Jews will be killed (Zechariah 13:8-9). This is the time both Jeremiah and Daniel refer to as a time of unparalleled "distress" for the Jewish people (Jeremiah 30:7 and Daniel 12:1). And so it will be. Here's how the prophet Zephaniah describes it (Zephaniah 1:14-17):

> 14) Near is the great day of the LORD, near and coming very quickly; listen, the day of the LORD! In it the warrior cries out bitterly.
>
> 15) A day of wrath is that day, a day of trouble and distress, a day of destruction and desolation, a day of darkness and gloom, a day of clouds and thick darkness,
>
> 16) a day of trumpet and battle cry against the fortified cities and the high corner towers.
>
> 17) I will bring distress on men so that they will walk like the blind, because they have sinned against the LORD; and their blood will be poured out like dust and their flesh like dung.

In the midst of those terrible days, the Jewish people will cry out with the words of Psalm 70:1-2:

> 1) O God, hasten to deliver me; O LORD, hasten to my help!
>
> 2) Let those be ashamed and humiliated who seek my life; let those be turned back and dishonored who delight in my hurt.

Why will Satan motivate the Antichrist to focus his wrath on the Jewish people? It's because, as I have pointed out before, Satan hates the Jews with a passion because:

- They are God's Chosen People.
- It was through the Jews that God gave the Scriptures.
- It was through the Jews that God provided the Messiah, Jesus.
- God has promised that one day a great remnant of the Jews will accept Jesus as their Messiah (Isaiah 10:22, Romans 9:27 and 11:25-27).

Again, as I have pointed out before, Satan wants to annihilate the Chosen People of God so that God cannot keep His promise that one day a great remnant of the Jews will turn their hearts to His Son and be saved.

The Purpose of the "Great Tribulation"

But why is God going to allow this carnage to occur? The answer is one that is hard to swallow. He is going to work through the suffering of a Second Holocaust to bring the Jewish people to the end of themselves so that they will turn their hardened hearts to God, receive His Son as their Messiah, and be saved.

The Scriptures portray this horrific experience in allegorical language, describing it as a refining process (Ezekiel 22:18-22):

> 18) "Son of man, the house of Israel has become dross to Me; all of them are bronze and tin and iron and lead in the furnace; they are the dross of silver.
>
> 19) "Therefore, thus says the Lord GOD, 'Because all of you have become dross, therefore, behold, I am going to gather you into the midst of Jerusalem.

> 20) 'As they gather silver and bronze and iron and lead and tin into the furnace to blow fire on it in order to melt it, so I will gather you in My anger and in My wrath and I will lay you there and melt you.
>
> 21) 'I will gather you and blow on you with the fire of My wrath, and you will be melted in the midst of it.
>
> 22) 'As silver is melted in the furnace, so you will be melted in the midst of it; and you will know that I, the LORD, have poured out My wrath on you.'"

Malachi, the last prophet of the Hebrew Scriptures, uses the same imagery. Speaking of the Messiah, he says (Malachi 3:2-4):

> 2) "But who can endure the day of His coming? And who can stand when He appears? For He is like a refiner's fire and like fullers' soap.
>
> 3) "He will sit as a smelter and purifier of silver, and He will purify the sons of Levi and refine them like gold and silver, so that they may present to the LORD offerings in righteousness.
>
> 4) "Then the offering of Judah and Jerusalem will be pleasing to the LORD as in the days of old and as in former years."

In one verse, the prophet Zechariah sums up the process and its results, using the same imagery. Speaking of the one-third of the Jews that will survive to the end of the Tribulation, he says, "And I will bring the third part through the fire, refine them as silver is refined, and test them as gold is tested" (Zechariah 13:9).

A Glorious Day of Salvation

Zechariah uses powerful language to describe in detail the repentance and salvation of the Jewish remnant that will take place on the day that Jesus returns to this earth (Zechariah 12:10):

> I will pour out on the house of David and on the inhabitants of Jerusalem, the Spirit of grace and of supplication, so that they will look on Me whom they have pierced; and they will mourn for Him, as one mourns for an only son, and they will weep bitterly over Him like the bitter weeping over a firstborn.

God's gracious response to this repentance is presented by Zechariah in the next chapter: "In that day a fountain will be opened for the house of David and for the inhabitants of Jerusalem, for sin and for impurity" (Zechariah 13:1).

Isaiah tells us that after this marvelous day of salvation has taken place, God will look back upon it and say (Isaiah 54:7-8):

> 7) "For a brief moment I forsook you, but with great compassion I will gather you.
>
> 8) "In an outburst of anger I hid My face from you for a moment, but with everlasting lovingkindness I will have compassion on you," says the LORD your Redeemer.

IV. The Regathering in Belief

When Yeshua returns to this earth, in what Christians call the Second Coming (Hebrews 9:28), He will gather all the surviving and believing Jews left in the world to their homeland of Israel.

There have already been two regatherings of the Jews to Israel. The first was after their Babylonian captivity. This regathering began in 536 BC when Cyrus, the King of Persia, agreed to allow the Jews captured by the Babylonians to return to Jerusalem. The second began at the end of the 19th Century when Jews responded to Theodor Herzl's vision of a re-established homeland by making aliyah to what was then called Palestine. This regathering continued throughout the 20th Century.

The Last Regathering

The third regathering at the end of the Tribulation will be very different, for it will be a regathering in belief. It was first prophesied by Moses in the last speech he gave to the Children of Israel before they entered their Promised Land (Deuteronomy 30:1-5):

> 1) "So it shall be when all of these things have come upon you, the blessing and the curse which I have set before you, and you call them to mind in all nations where the LORD your God has banished you,
>
> 2) and you return to the LORD your God and obey Him with all your heart and soul according to all that I command you today, you and your sons,
>
> 3) then the LORD your God will restore you from captivity, and have compassion on you, and will gather you again from all the peoples where the LORD your God has scattered you.
>
> 4) "If your outcasts are at the ends of the earth, from there the LORD your God will gather you, and from there He will bring you back.
>
> 5) "The LORD your God will bring you into the land which your fathers possessed, and you shall possess it; and He will prosper you

> and multiply you more than your fathers."

Many years later, the prophet Ezekiel beautifully described in detail the tender love of God that will prompt Him to bring about this regathering in belief (Ezekiel 34:11-16):

> 11) For thus says the Lord GOD, "Behold, I Myself will search for My sheep and seek them out.
>
> 12) "As a shepherd cares for his herd in the day when he is among his scattered sheep, so I will care for My sheep and will deliver them from all the places to which they were scattered on a cloudy and gloomy day.
>
> 13) "I will bring them out from the peoples and gather them from the countries and bring them to their own land; and I will feed them on the mountains of Israel, by the streams, and in all the inhabited places of the land.
>
> 14) "I will feed them in a good pasture, and their grazing ground will be on the mountain heights of Israel. There they will lie down on good grazing ground and feed in rich pasture on the mountains of Israel.
>
> 15) "I will feed My flock and I will lead them to rest," declares the Lord GOD.
>
> 16) "I will seek the lost, bring back the scattered, bind up the broken and strengthen the sick; but the fat and the strong I will destroy. I will feed them with judgment."

Isaiah describes the incredible joy that will be evidenced by this remnant that has found their Messiah and is regathered to their homeland (Isaiah 35:10):

> And the ransomed of the LORD will return and come with joyful shouting to Zion, with everlasting joy upon their heads. They will find gladness and joy, and sorrow and sighing will flee away.

V. Spiritual Regeneration

The prophets make it clear that this third and final regathering of the Jewish people will consist of those who have been spiritually regenerated by accepting Yeshua (Jesus) as their Messiah.

Again, Moses said this regathering would not occur until "you [the Jewish people] return to the LORD your God and obey Him with all your heart and soul . . ." (Deuteronomy 30:2). Moses further stated that this would be the time when "God will circumcise your heart . . . to love the LORD your God with all your heart and with all your soul" (Deuteronomy 30:6).

In like manner, Ezekiel asserted that when this regathering takes place, God will "sprinkle clean water" on the Jewish people, and they will be cleansed from all their "filthiness and idols" (Ezekiel 36:25). Ezekiel continues, speaking for the Lord (Ezekiel 36;26-28):

> 26) "Moreover, I will give you a new heart and put a new spirit within you; and I will remove the heart of stone from your flesh and give you a heart of flesh.
>
> 27) "I will put My Spirit within you and cause you to walk in My statutes, and you will be careful to observe My ordinances.
>
> 28) "You will live in the land that I gave to your forefathers; so you will be My people, and I will be your God."

VI. A New Covenant

At that time, the Jewish people will be brought into a new relationship with God. It will be one that is based on a New Covenant — the covenant that came into being at the death of Jesus.

Ezekiel refers to it as "an everlasting covenant" (Ezekiel 16:60) and a "covenant of peace" (Ezekiel 34:25 and 37:26).

The most detailed description of this New Covenant is given by the prophet Jeremiah (Jeremiah 31:31-34):

> 31) "Behold, days are coming," declares the LORD, "when I will make a new covenant with the house of Israel and with the house of Judah,
>
> 32) not like the covenant which I made with their fathers in the day I took them by the hand to bring them out of the land of Egypt, My covenant which they broke, although I was a husband to them," declares the LORD.
>
> 33) "But this is the covenant which I will make with the house of Israel after those days," declares the LORD, "I will put My law within them and on their heart I will write it; and I will be their God, and they shall be My people.
>
> 34) "They will not teach again, each man his neighbor and each man his brother, saying, 'Know the LORD,' for they will all know Me, from the least of them to the greatest of them," declares the LORD, "for I will forgive their iniquity, and their sin I will remember no more."

Again, Jeremiah is speaking of the New Covenant that became valid at the death of Jesus. The writer of the New Testament book of Hebrews affirmed this truth in Hebrews 9:15 when he stated that Jesus "is the mediator of a new covenant . . ." He also asserted that this new covenant "has made the first obsolete" (Hebrews 8:13).

VII. The Millennium & Primacy

After all the Jewish believers on planet Earth are regathered to Israel, Jesus will inaugurate His millennial reign by making them the prime nation on earth. In the process, He will fulfill all the promises that have been madc to the Jewish people in their Scriptures.

The blessings they will receive are simply mind-boggling. The prophet Isaiah outlines them in detail in three chapters — 60 through 62. He begins by proclaiming, "Arise, shine, for your light [the Messiah] has come and the glory of the LORD has risen upon you" (Isaiah 60:1). He then proceeds to list the specific blessings the Jewish people will receive:

- Israel will be the prime nation on the earth — a literal light to all the other nations, for the Lord's Shekinah Glory will rest upon the nation. (Isaiah 60:3).
- The wealth of the nations will be given to Israel (Isaiah 60:5,10,16 and Isaiah 61:6).
- A glorious new Temple will be provided (Isaiah 60:7,13).
- The nation of Israel will enjoy peace (Isaiah 60:11,17-18).
- The land of Israel will be reclaimed, receiving "the glory of Lebanon" (Isaiah 60:13).

- The Lord Himself will dwell in Jerusalem, and it will be called "the city of the LORD," meaning "The City of Yahweh" (Isaiah 60:13-14,19).
- The Jewish people will receive respect worldwide, becoming "an everlasting pride and a joy from generation to generation" (Isaiah 60:15).
- The land of Israel — all that has ever been promised (Genesis 15:18-21) — will be given to the Jewish people to possess forever (Isaiah 60:21).
- The Jewish people will receive a garland of gladness and a mantle of praise (Isaiah 61:3,7,10).
- All the ancient ruins of Israel will be rebuilt (Isaiah 61:4).
- The Jewish people will serve as "priests of the Lord" and will be spoken of as "ministers of God" (Isaiah 61:6).
- The Jewish people will receive a new "everlasting" covenant with the Lord (Isaiah 61:8-9).

Renewal of Jerusalem

Isaiah concludes this remarkable series of chapters by focusing on what the Lord is going to do with Jerusalem. He says the city will be "a crown of beauty in the hand of the LORD" (Isaiah 62:3). It will be a glorious place of righteousness (Isaiah 62:2). And it will be "a praise in the earth" (Isaiah 62:7).

Isaiah also says that Jerusalem will be given a new name (Isaiah 62:2), but he does not reveal that name. However, the prophet Ezekiel does. He says it will be "Yahweh Shemmah." which means, "The Lord is There" (Ezekiel 48:35).

The Primacy of Israel

And He certainly will be. Isaiah says the Messiah will reign over all the world from Jerusalem as King of kings and Lord of lords (Isaiah 2:1-4). Ezekiel tells us that David in his resurrected glorified body will reign as King of Israel (Ezekiel 34:23-24). Daniel says that all the saints in glorified bodies (both Jew and Gentile) will reign with the Messiah worldwide, ruling over the saved Gentiles who lived to the end of the Tribulation and were allowed to enter the Millennium in the flesh to repopulate the earth (Daniel 7:13-14,18, 27).

The blessings of God are going to flow out to the nations of the world through the Jewish people, and they will be given the honor and respect they deserve as the Chosen People of God — something they have been denied throughout their history. Whereas today they are vilified, persecuted and mistreated in every imaginable way, during the thousand year reign of Jesus, they will be so respected, that when a Jew walks by, ten Gentiles will grab his robe and say, "Let us go with you, for we have heard that God is with you" (Zechariah 8:23).

VIII. Conclusion

Looking back over the prophecies concerning the Jewish people that God has already fulfilled, and considering the yet to be fulfilled prophecies, I am overwhelmed by God's passionate love for the Jewish people.

Any god created by the mind of Man would have washed his hands of the Jewish people long ago. Only the true Creator God of Grace would continue to love them and pursue them despite their stubborn rebellion against Him.

But then, that is true of each one of us, both Gentile and Jew. There is not a single person on planet Earth today who deserves God's love and the salvation that He offers through the blood of His Son. All of us have sinned and fallen short of the glory of God (Romans 3:9-23).

The Jewish people were selected by God to be His Chosen People, and they still are. That does not mean they are automatically saved. Rather, it means they were selected to be a witness of the One True God to the world (Deuteronomy 7:6-9 and Isaiah 43:10-12).

When they failed to accept their Messiah, God placed them under discipline, where they remain to this day. But they also remain a witness of God's unfathomable grace. He has promised that despite their rejection of His Son, He intends to pursue them to the point of their repentance, at which time a great remnant of them will be forgiven and sealed for redemption.

The End Time Plan

Today, we can see God putting His end time plan for Israel into action:

- He has returned them to their land and their capital city of Jerusalem, just as He promised.
- He is now bringing all the nations of the world against them, just as was prophesied.
- They will soon be placed in a refining fire during the Tribulation — again, just as has been prophesied.
- Through the intense suffering of their "time of distress," they will be brought to the end of themselves.
- And when their Messiah bursts from the heavens, they will repent and cry out, "Blessed is He who comes in the Name of the LORD!"

Jesus Himself told his disciples during the last week of His life on this earth that He would not return until the Jewish people were willing to cry out, "Baruch Haba B'Shem Adonai!" (Matthew 23:39).

The Salvation of the Remnant

When the Jewish people turn to God in repentance, He will forgive and forget and receive them home to Him like a prodigal son, once again demonstrating His glorious grace. All of which motivated the Apostle Paul to cry out, "Oh, the depth of the riches both of the wisdom and knowledge of God! How unsearchable are His judgments and unfathomable His ways!" (Romans 11:33).

In like manner, the entire redeemed Jewish nation will be filled with joy beyond anything they have ever experienced. It is on that day they will exclaim (Psalm 98:1-3):

> 1) O sing to the LORD a new song, for He has done wonderful things, His right hand and His holy arm have gained the victory for Him.
>
> 2) The LORD has made known His salvation; He has revealed His righteousness in the sight of the nations.
>
> 3) He has remembered His lovingkindness and His faithfulness to the house of Israel; all the ends of the earth have seen the salvation of our God.

My earnest prayer is that this day will be realized in history very soon.

MARANATHA! (1 Corinthians 16:22)

Epilogue

As we look back over all the prophecies God has fulfilled regarding the Jewish people and — and is still in the process of fulfilling — a fundamental question emerges: "What is the significance of this to Christians living at the beginning of the 21st Century?"

Well, there are many reasons that the fulfillment of end time prophecies about Israel are important to the Church.

Proof of the Bible

To begin with, the fulfillment of ancient prophecies about Israel in these end times is proof positive that the Bible is of supernatural origin. How else could it possibly be explained?

The prophecies are very precise in their meaning, and their fulfillments have been just as precise. This cannot be a coincidence. The exact fulfillment of so many prophecies is beyond the realm of happenstance.

The Bible is the only book that contains fulfilled prophecies, and it contains hundreds concerning towns, nations, empires, individuals and the Messiah. No other book can match this. There are no fulfilled prophecies in the Qur'an, the Book of Mormon or the Hindu Vedas.

The world says the Bible is Man's search for God and is therefore full of myths, legends and superstitions. Fulfilled prophecies concerning both the Messiah and Israel prove otherwise. They establish the fact that the Bible is God's revelation to Mankind.

Proof of God

The truth that the Bible is of supernatural origin points to the fact that there is a God who superintended the writing.

All my life I have heard people say, "You can't prove God's existence. You just have to accept it by faith." I have even heard this proclaimed from the pulpit.

That is nonsense, for there is all kinds of evidence of the existence of God, one of the greatest being the incredible design of our universe, our planet and our bodies. Design demands a designer. Design does not happen by chance.

To say, as Evolutionists do, that everything came into existence from a "Big Bang" followed by evolution is pure fantasy. How many explosions have you ever witnessed that produced order instead of chaos? Evolution is akin to arguing that a Boeing 747 is the accidental product of a tornado blowing through a junk yard — or contending that the images carved on Mount Rushmore are the accidental result of natural erosion.

In like manner, fulfilled prophecy shouts the existence of God. This point was made by the prophet Isaiah when he attacked idolatry among the Jewish people (Isaiah 41:21-23, LBP):

> 21) "Can your idols make such claims as these? Let them come and show what they can do!" says God, the King of Israel.
>
> 22) "Let them try to tell us what occurred in years gone by or what the future holds.
>
> 23) "Yes, that's it! If you are gods, tell what will happen in the days ahead! Or do some mighty miracle that makes us stare, amazed."

In other words, if the totem pole you are worshiping is truly God, then ask it to tell you what is going to happen in the future. Only the true God can do that, and the only true God is Yahweh, the author of all Bible prophecies.

The Faithfulness of God

A third reason fulfilled Bible prophecies concerning Israel are important to the Church is because they are a demonstration of the faithfulness of God to His promises.

King Solomon emphasized this truth in a prayer he prayed at the dedication of the First Temple. He began the prayer with these words: "O LORD, the God of Israel, there is no god like You in heaven or on earth, keeping covenant and showing lovingkindness to Your servants who walk before You with all their heart . . ." (1 Kings 8:23).

Yes, the true God of this universe is a covenant and promise keeping God who is always true to His Word. This is clearly demonstrated in His fulfillment of the prophetic promises to the Jewish people that were made by their God-given prophets thousands of years ago.

This should be a source of hope to Christians because God has made many promises to the Church, and as we witness Him fulfilling all the promises He has made to Israel, we can be certain that He will likewise fulfill all the promises He has made to the Church.

And those promises are nothing less than sensational. We have been promised through God's prophets that one day very soon, Jesus will appear in the heavens for His Church and will take us out of this world before God pours out His wrath in the Great Tribulation. We have also been promised that we will be given glorified bodies that will be immortal in nature and that we will return to this earth with Jesus at the end of the Tribulation to reign with Him during His millennial rule over this earth.

Further, we have been promised that at the end of His reign, we will be taken off this earth again and placed in the

New Jerusalem He is now preparing for us, from which we will witness this earth consumed by fire to burn away the pollution of Satan's last revolt. Out of that fiery inferno will come a New Earth on which we will live eternally in the New Jerusalem in the presence of our Creator who will come to earth to live in our midst (Revelation 21:1-7).

The Meaning of Grace

The fourth reason fulfilled prophecy regarding Israel is important to the Church is one that I have alluded to throughout this book — it is a glorious demonstration of the meaning of God's grace.

No false god created by the mind of Man would tolerate the Jewish people. Just think about their history. They murmured constantly against God and Moses after their deliverance from Egyptian captivity — and they continued to do so even after experiencing one miracle after another during their pilgrimage to the Promise Land. Then, after their entrance into the land, they continued to rebel against God's commands until they ultimately gave their hearts over to idolatry.

Moses called them a "stubborn" and "rebellious" people (Deuteronomy 9: 6-7). In Psalm 78, the prophet Asaph spoke of their behavior as they wandered in the wilderness after their exodus from Egypt:

> "they put God to the test" (verse 18).
> "they did not believe in God" (verse 22).
> "they did not trust in His salvation" (verse 22).
> "they did not believe in His wonderful works" (verse 32).
> "they tempted God" (verse 41).
> "they did not remember His power" (verse 42).

Jeremiah referred to the Jewish people over and over again as a people who had "stiffened their necks" against God (Jeremiah 7:26, 17:23 and 19:15). And in the New Testament, when one of the first Jewish converts, a man named Stephen, presented an oration about the history of Israel, he characterized his people as "stiff-necked and uncircumcised in heart and ears . . . always resisting the Holy Spirit . . . doing just as your fathers did" (Acts 7:51). His audience responded by stoning him to death (Acts 7:57-60).

God Himself referred to His Chosen People as "stubborn and obstinate" (Ezekiel 2:4). But God also repeatedly affirmed His love for them. In Jeremiah 31:36 God says the Jewish people will continue to be "a nation before Me forever." He emphasizes the point by saying they will continue as a special nation of people until the fixed order of the universe ceases, or until all the heavens and ocean depths have been measured (Jeremiah 31:36-37). In Isaiah 49:14-16 God uses a different metaphor to emphasize His devotion to Israel. He says that He has the nation inscribed on the palms of His hands! He also says that those who touch the Jewish people, touch the apple of His eye (Zechariah 2:8).

There are three chapters in the New Testament that strongly emphasize the continuing love of God for the Jews. These three chapters have been despised and ignored (or spiritualized into meaninglessness) throughout much of Christian history. The chapters are Romans 9-11. In Romans 9:4 Paul writes that God still has covenants with the Jews which He promises to fulfill. He then makes it clear that the Jews who will receive the blessings are a great remnant that will be saved in the end times (Romans 9:27).

Paul even specifically addresses the question of whether or not God has rejected the Jewish people. He asks, "God has not rejected His people has He?" (Romans 11:1). For 1600 years the Church has answered this question with an unqualified, "Yes!" But Paul answers it by saying, "May it never be!… God has not rejected His people whom he foreknew" (Romans 11:1-2).

But what about their disobedience? What about their rejection of God as king of their nation and Jesus as king of their hearts? Hasn't their disobedience nullified the promises of God? Again, Paul specifically deals with this issue. He asks, "What then? If some did not believe, their unbelief will not nullify the faithfulness of God, will it?" (Romans 3:3). And again, for centuries the Church has responded, "Yes!" But not Paul. He responds by saying, "May it never be! Rather, let God be found true, though every man be found a liar" (Romans 3:4).

What a glorious demonstration of the meaning of grace as unmerited love! Even today, after their miraculous regathering from the four corners of the earth, the Jewish people persist in their unbelief and rebellion. And yet God continues to love them and protect them and orchestrate history toward the day of their salvation.

When I first started preaching about God's love for the Jewish people and his absolute determination to bring a great remnant to salvation despite their stubbornness and rebellion, my wife said, "You make me want to be a Jew!" I responded by saying, "No, dear, you wouldn't want to be a Jew because the overwhelming odds are that you would have a spiritual veil that would keep you from recognizing Jesus as your Messiah (2 Corinthians 3:14-16).

I then pointed out to her that God is not doing one thing for the Jewish people that He is not willing to do for anyone. The Jews, again, are simply a witness of God's desire for all people to come to repentance and be saved (2 Peter 3:9). God does not "wash His hands" of anyone. He pursues and pursues, trying to bring us to the end of ourselves so that we will turn to Him in repentance and be saved. That is exactly what is going to happen to the Jewish remnant at the end of the Tribulation. Here's how the prophet Malachi put it in Malachi 3:

> 2) "But who can endure the day of His coming? And who can stand when He appears? For He is like a refiner's fire and like fullers' soap.
>
> 3) "He will sit as a smelter and purifier of silver, and He will purify the sons of Levi and refine them like gold and silver, so that they may present to the LORD offerings in righteousness.
>
> 4) "Then the offering of Judah and Jerusalem will be pleasing to the LORD as in the days of old and as in former years."

The Jewish people are witnesses of what it means to have a relationship with God. Their history shows that when you are obedient to God's Word, He blesses. When you rebel, He disciplines. And when you repent, He forgives and forgets and blesses again. But He never gives up on us. He is a pursuer of souls, and His abiding relationship with Israel is proof of it. That's what grace is all about.

The Return of the Messiah

The final reason I would argue that Israel in Bible prophecy is relevant to the Church is because it is one of the strongest evidences that we are living in the season of the Messiah's return.

The regathering of the Jewish people, the re-establishment of their state, and their reoccupation of the city of Jerusalem are all end time prophecies, and their fulfillment is a trumpet blast announcing that we are on the threshold of the Tribulation and that Jesus is at the very gates of Heaven awaiting for His Father's command to return for His Church.

Accordingly, the fulfillment of these prophecies made to Israel should be a wake-up call to the Church, causing us to face up to the reality that we are living on borrowed time, and we therefore need to commit ourselves to holiness and evangelism.

The whole world is coming against Israel, just as prophesied (Zechariah 12:1-3). The whole world is descending into chaos, just as prophesied (Matthew 24:37-39). The signs of the times are shouting the Messiah's soon return.

Jesus said that would not happen until the Jewish people are willing to shout, "Blessed is He who comes in the name of the Lord!" (Matthew 23:39). The Bible says that will happen when the Jewish remnant comes to the end of itself at the end of the Tribulation and turns to God in repentance.

Crucial Questions

What about you? Are you ready for the Lord's return? If He were to appear in the heavens today for His Church, would you be taken in the Rapture, or would you be left behind to face the Antichrist?

The Bible says that those who are ready for the Lord's return will welcome Him with the joy of "calves released from a stall" (Malachi 4:2). But those who are not ready will become ashes under the soles of His feet (Malachi 4:3).

Swallow your pride, confess you are a sinner, reach out in faith to God and receive His Son as your Lord and Savior (John 3:16). Then seek out a body of believers where you can publicly confess your faith and manifest it in baptism. And where you can begin to grow in the Lord through a systematic study of His Word.

And never forget that God will be as faithful, loving and compassionate toward you as He has been toward the Jewish people.

Conclusion

When the Jewish people returned to their homeland from Babylonian captivity, the Levitical priests gathered them, read the Word of God to them, called on them to repent, and then "cried with a loud voice," reminding them that they and their forefathers had refused to listen to God and did not remember His wondrous deeds (Nehemiah 9:17).

They then reminded the people that the only reason they had been allowed to return home was because their God, Yahweh, is "a God of forgiveness, gracious and compassionate, slow to anger and abounding in lovingkindness . . ."

Hallelujah!

References

Prologue:

1) The date of the beginning of the Exodus is based on 1 Kings 6:1 which reads: "Now it came about in the four hundred and eightieth year after the sons of Israel came out of the land of Egypt, in the fourth year of Solomon's reign over Israel, in the month of Ziv which is the second month, that he began to build the house of the LORD." This verse gives a time period of 480 years between the Exodus and the beginning of Solomon's work on the Jerusalem Temple. From John Bright's chronology in *A History of Israel* (1959), Solomon ascended to the throne around 961 BC, which would make the fourth year of his reign and the beginning of temple construction about 959-957 BC. Working backward from this date, we arrive at a date around 1440 BC for the Exodus. The specific dates used throughout this book are taken from "The Bible Timeline" that can be found at biblehub.com.

2) Jeroboam's original alternative worship center was established in the central hill country and was called Shechem (I Kings 12:25). Fifty-seven years later, the capital of the kingdom of Israel was moved to the city of Samaria during the reign of King Omri (1 Kings 16:23-24).

Chapter 1: Dispersion of the Jews

1) The Canadian film producer, Simcha Jacobovici, found remnants of the tribes of Israel scattered all across Eurasia and presented his evidence in a 2003 documentary film titled, "Quest for the Lost Tribes." Unlike the Babylonians who kept their captives confined to one area, the Assyrians scattered theirs into small pockets located all across the Middle East. See: Jewish Virtual Library, "The Two Kingdoms of Israel (c. 920 BCE - 587 BCE)," www.jewishvirtual library.org/jsource/History/Kingdoms1.html.

2) Jewish Virtual Library, "The Diaspora," www.jewishvirtuallibrary.org/jsource/History/Diaspora.html, page 1.

3) Shaye I. D. Cohen, "The Jewish Diaspora," www.pbs.org/wgbh/pages/frontline/shows/religion/portrait/diaspora.html, page 4.

4) L. Michael White, "The Jewish Diaspora," www.pbs.org/wgbh/

pages/frontline/shows/religion/portrait/diaspora. html, page 1. See also: Encyclopedia Britannica, "Diaspora," www.britannica.com/EBchedked/topic/161756/Diaspora, page 1.

5) Encyclopedia Britannica, "Diaspora," www.britannica.com/EB checked/topic/161756/Diaspora, page 1.

6) Jewish Virtual Library, "Ancient Jewish History: Roman Rule (63 BCE - 313 CE)," www.jewishvirtuallibrary.org/jsource/History/Romans.html, page 1.

7) Jewish Virtual Library: "Ancient Jewish History: The Revolt (66 - 70 CE)," www.jewishvirtuallibary.org/ jsource/Judaism/revolt.html, page 1.

8) Ibid.

9) Cassius Dio (translation by Earnest Cary), *Roman History*, book 69, 12.1 - 14.3, http://penelope.uchicago.edu/Thayer/E/Roman/Texts/Cassius_Dio/69*.html.

10) "Aelia Capitolina," www.welcometohosanna.com/JERU SALEM_TOUR/aeliacap.htm, page 2.

11) Ibid.

12) Joseph Bickersteth Mayor, *Epistle of St. James: The Greek Text with Introduction, Notes and Comments* (Macmillan, 1897), page cxiv, https://books.google.com/books?id=Lu0UAAAAYAAJ&dq=there+is+no+city,+no+tribe,+whether+Greek+or+barbaria&source=gbs_navlinks_s.

13) Shira Schoenberg, "Judaism: The Ashkenazim," www.jewishvir tuallibrary.org/jsource/Judaism/Askenazim.html..

14) Rebecca Walker, "Judaism: The Sephardim," www.jewishvirtual library.org/jsource/Judaism/Sephardim.html.

15) Wikipedia, "Mizrahi Jews," http://en.wikipedia.org/wiki/Mizrahi_Jews.

16) Haim Hillel Ben-Sasson, "Anusim," www.jewishvirtuallibrary.org/jsource/judaica/ejud_0002_0002_0_01173.html.

17) Shira Schoenberg, page 1.

18) Judaism 101, "Yiddish Language and Culture," www.jewfaq.org/yiddish.htm.

19) Shelomo Alfassa, "A Quick Explanation of Ladino (Judeo-Spanish)," www.sephardicstudies.org/quickladino.html.

20) Loolwa Khazzoom, ""Ancient Jewish History: Jews of the Middle East," www.jewishvirtuallibrary.org/jsource/Judaism/mejews.html. See also: Benjamin Hary, "Judeo-Arabic," www.jewish-languages.org/judeo-arabic.html.

21) Daniel J. Elazar, "Land, State, and Diaspora in the History of the Jewish Polity," www.jcpa.org/dje/articles/land-stat-polity.htm, page 14.

22) Ibid.

23) Jewish Virtual Library, "Vital Statistics: Jewish Population of the World (1882 - Present)," www.jewishvirtuallibrary.org/jsource/Judaism/jewpop.html.

24) Rabbi Kalman Packouz, "7 Wonders of Jewish History," www.simpletoremember.com/articles/a/7-wonders-of-jewish-history, page 4.

25) David R. Reagan, *America the Beautiful? The United States in Bible Prophecy*, (McKinney, TX: Lamb & Lion Ministries, 3rd edition, 2009).

Chapter 2: Persecution of the Jews

1) For an in-depth, detailed discussion of the evils of Replacement Theology, see Dr. Reagan's book, *The Jewish People: Rejected or Beloved?* (McKinney, TX: Lamb & Lion Ministries, 2014).

2) It is generally assumed that Luke, who wrote the Gospel of Luke and the book of Acts, was a Gentile, but this is probably incorrect. For evidence that Luke was a Jew, see: Tom McCall, "Was Luke a Gentile?" *Lamplighter* magazine, September-October 2007, pages 12-13.

3) Reuven Efraim Schmalz and Raymond Robert Fischer, *The Messianic Seal of the Jerusalem Church* (Olin Publications: Tiberias, Israel, 2nd edition, 1999).

4) There are several good summaries on the Internet of the anti-Semitism of the early Church Fathers. See, for example:

   a) YashaNet, "Anti-Semitism of the 'Church Fathers,'" www.yashanet.com/library/fathers.htm.

   b) Anonymous, "The History of the Church in Relation to Israel," http://fp.thebeers.f9.co.uk/history.htm.

   c) Wikipedia, "Christianity and Anti-Semitism," http://en.wikipe

dia.org/wiki/Christianity_and_antisemitism.

There are also some good timeline summaries of Christian anti-Semitism:

a) www.answers.com/topic/timeline-of-antisemitism.

b) www.religioustolerance.org/jud_pers1.htm.

5) John G. Gager, *The Origins of Anti-Semitism* (London: Oxford University Press, 1983), pp. 127-129.

6) Centre for the Study of Historical Christian Antisemitism, "Justin Martyr," www.hcacentre.org/JustinMartyr.html.

7) LeadershipU, "The Jews as the Christians Saw Them," www.leaderu.com/ftissues/ft9705/articles/wilken. html.

8) John T. Pawlikowski, *Journal of Religion & Society*, "Christian Anti-Semitism: Past History, Present Challenges," http://moses.creighton.edu/JRS/2004/2004-10.html.

9) Centre for the Study of Historical Christian Antisemitism, "Origen," www.hcacentre.org/Origen.html.

10) California State University at Northridge, "Canons of the Church Council at Elvira (Granada) ca. 309 AD," www.csun.edu/~hcfll004/elvira.html.

11) New Advent, "Easter Controversy," www.newadvent.org/cathen/05228a.htm.

12) Gene Shaparenko, "The Resurgence of 'Christian' Anti-Semitism," www.aquatechnology.net/RESURGENCE.html.

13) Centre for the Study of Historical Christian Antisemitism, "John Chrysostom," www.hcacentre.org/JohnChrysostom.html.

14) Ibid., "St. Jerome," www.hcacentre.org/Jerome.html.

15) Ibid., "Saint Augustine," www.hcacentre.org/Augustine.html.

16) John Weiss, *Ideology of Death: Why the Holocaust Happened in Germany*, (Chicago: Ivan R. Dee, 1996) p. 15.

17) Florida Holocaust Museum, "Antisemitism," www.flholocaustmuseum.org/history_wing/antisemitism/crusades.cfm.

18) ReligiousTolerance.org., "Blood Libel Myths: Then and Now," www.religioustolerance.org/jud_blib1.htm.

19) Remember.org., "Classical and Christian Anti-Semitism," www.remember.org/History.root.classical.html.

20) Jewish History Sourcebook, "The Expulsion from Spain, 1492 CE," www.fordham.edu/halsall/jewish/1492-jews-spain1.html.

21) The Jewish Virtual Library, "Martin Luther: The Jews and Their Lies (1543)," www.jewishvirtuallibrary.org/jsource/anti-semitism/Luther_on_Jews.html.

22) Phyllis Petty, "Christian Hatred and Persecution of the Jews," www.therefinersfire.org/antisemitism_in_church.htm.

23) Ibid.

24) Ibid.

25) Knox Theological Seminary, "An Open Letter to Evangelicals and Other Interested Parties: The People of God, the Land of Israel, and the Impartiality of the Gospel," www.knoxseminary.org/Prospective/Faculty/WittenbergDoor/index.html.

26) Ibid., introduction.

27) Ibid., section IV.

28) Ibid., section IX.

29) Ibid., conclusion.

30) Jan Jaben-Eilon, "Messianic Jewish groups claim rapid growth," June 12, 2012, http://jewishjournal.com/religion/105069.

31) *The Qur'an,* Sura 5:60.

32) Wikipedia, "Antisemitism in Japan," https://en.wikipedia.org/wiki/Antisemitism_in_Japan.

Chapter 3: Preservation of the Jews

1) Rabbi Kalman Packouz, "7 Wonders of Jewish History," www.simpletoremember.com/articles/a/7-wonders-of-jewish-history, page 1.

2) William Varner, "The Preservation of the Jewish People," www.foi.org, page 2.

3) Anonymous, "9 Great Quotes About Jews by Non-Jews," www.aish.com, page 1.

4) Ibid.

5) Dov Greenburg, "The Science of Jewish Survival," www.chabad.org, page 1,

6) Mark Twain, "The Secret of Jewish Survival," www.shomreitorah.org, page 2.

7) Virtual Jerusalem, "10 of the Greatest Quotes About Israel and the Jews," www.virtualjerusalem.com/culture.php?Itemid=11334, page 1.

8) Varner, page 2.

9) For details about the persecution of the Jews during the Middle Ages, see Dr. David Reagan's book, *The Jewish People: Rejected or Beloved?* (McKinney, TX: Lamb & Lion Ministries, 2014), pages 93-124.

10) Rabbi Dovid Gottlieb, "Jewish Survival – The Fact and its Implications," www.ohr.edu/2055, page 3.

11) Prioktan918, "How did Judaism survive the Diaspora?" www.answers.com/Q/How_did_judaism_survive_the diaspora, page 1.

12) Ibid.

13) Gottlieb, page 6.

14) Nissan Dovid Dubov, "What is the Secret of Jewish Survival?" www.chabad.org., page 2.

15) Tracy R. Rich, "A List of the 613 Mitzvot (Commandments)," www.jewfaq.org/613.htm, page 1.

16) Tracey R. Rich, "Halakhah: Jewish Law," www.jewfaq.org/hala khah.htm, pages 1-4.

17) Greenburg, page 2.

18) Ibid., page 3.

19) Ibid., page 2.

20) John J. Parsons, "The Jewish Holidays: A Simplified Overview of the Feasts of the LORD," www.hebrew4christians.com.

21) Packouz, page 3.

22) Wikipedia, "Demographics of China," https://en.wikipedia.org/Demographics_of_China, page 2.

23) Wikipedia, "Arabs," https://en.widipedia.org/wiki/Arabs, page 1.

Chapter 4: Desolation of the Land

1) *Scientific American,* "50 Years Ago: The Reclamation of a Man-Made Desert," April 1960, www.scientificamerican.com.
2) Dr. Jonathan Miesse, *A Journey to Egypt and Palestine in the Year 1855* (Chillicothe, Ohio: Scioto Gazette Office, 1859).
3) Miesse, page 157.
4) Mark Twain, *The Innocents Abroad* (Hartford, Connecticut: The American Publishing Co., 1860).
5) Twain, page 482.
6) Ibid., page 485
7) Ibid.
8) Ibid., page 520.
9) Ibid., page 555.
10) Ibid.
11) Ibid., page 606.
12) Ibid., pages 607-608.
13) Dr. Henry M. Field, *Among the Holy Hills* (New York: Charles Scribner's Sons, 1884), page 179.
14) Sir Frederick Treves, *The Land That Is Desolate: An Account of a Tour in Palestine* (London: Smith, Elder & Co., 1912).
15) Treves, page 21.
16) Ibid., page 33.
17) Ibid., page 40.
18) Ibid., page 120.
19) Ibid., page 177.
20) Ibid., page 193.
21) Ibid., pages 193, 196, 197.
22) Oliver C. Dalby, *Rambles in Scriptural Lands* (Self-published in 1924).
23) Dalby, page 91.

24) Rabbi Menachem Kohen, *Prophecies for the Era of Muslim Terror: A Torah Perspective on World Events* (Brooklyn, NY: Lambda Publishers, 2007).

25) Ibid., page 21.

26) Ibid., pages 28-33.

27) Israel Advocacy Movement, "Was Israel carved out of stolen land?" http://www.israeladvocacy.net/knowledge/the-truth-of-how-israel-was-created/was-israel-carved-out-of-stolen-land/#sthash.dLyeSQFh.dpbs.

Chapter 5: Regathering of the Jews

1) William I. Brustein , *Roots of Hate: Anti-Semitism in Europe Before the Holocaust,* (Cambridge, England: Cambridge University Press, 2003) page 119.

2) *The Jewish Encyclopedia*, "Drumont, Edouard Adolphe," www.jewishencyclopedia.com/articles/5336-drumont-edouard-adolphe.

3) Wikipedia, "La France Juive," http://en.wikipedia.org/wiki/Jewish_France.

4) Richard L. Rubinstein and John K. Roth, *Approaches to Auschwitz: The Holocaust and Its Legacy* (Louisville. Kentucky: Westminster John Knox Press, 2003), page 94.

5) The original title was *Der Judenstaat* (German for "The Jewish State"). It was published in 1896 in Leipzig and Vienna. Its subtitle was "A Proposal of a modern solution for the Jewish question."

6) Unsigned article published by the Zionism and Israel Information Center, "The Jewish State - 1896: Theodor Herzl's Program for Zionism," http://zionism-israel.com/Joshua/Jewish_State.html.

7) Jewish Virtual Library, "Immigration to Israel: The First Aliyah (1882-1903)," www.jewishvirtuallibrary.org/jsource/Immigration/First_Aliyah. html.

8) Jewish Virtual Library, "The Balfour Declaration: Commentary on the Declaration," www.jewishvirtuallibrary.org/jsource/History/balfour_commentary.html.

9) Jewish Virtual Library, "Demographics of Israel: Population of Israel/Palestine (1553 - Present)," www.jewishvirtuallibrary.org/jsource/History/demograhics.html.

10) Jewish Virtual Library, "Fact Sheet: Jewish Refugees from Arab Countries," www.jewishvirtuallibrary.org/jsource/talking/jewrefugees.htm.

11) Jewish Virtual Library, "Immigration to Israel: Total Immigration, from Former Soviet Union (1948 - Present)," www.jewishvirtuallibrary.org/jsource/Immigration/FSU.html.

12) Joel Brinkley, "Ethiopian Jews and Israelis Exult as Airlift Is Completed," *The New York Times*, May 26, 1991, www.nytimes.com/1991/05/26/world/ethiopian-jews-and-israelis-exult-as-airlift-is-completed.html.

Chapter 6: Re-establishment of the State

1) Connor Cruise O'Brien, *The Siege: The Saga of Israel and Zionism* (New York: Simon and Schuster, 1986), p. 272.

2) John Snetsinger, *Truman, the Jewish Vote and Israel* (Stanford, CA: Hoover Institution Press, 1974), p. 164.

3) O'Brien, p. 272.

4) Howard M. Sachar, *A History of Israel: From the Rise of Zionism to Our Time* (New York: Alfred A. Knopf, 1976), p. 284.

5) O'Brien, p. 274.

6) Sachar, pp. 284-285. See also O'Brien, p. 277.

7) Sachar, p. 292.

8) Ibid., p. 294.

9) David McCullough, *Truman* (New York: Simon & Schuster, 1992), p. 598.

10) Harry S. Truman, *Memoirs by Harry S. Truman: Years of Trial and Hope*, Volume 2 (Garden City, NY: Doubleday & Co., 1956), p. 157.

11) Truman, p. 159.

12) McCullough, p. 597.

13) Ibid., p. 602.

14) Ibid., p. 601.

15) Ibid., p. 611.

16) Sachar, p. 290.

17) Bernard Weisberger, "Interview with Clark Clifford," *American Heritage* magazine, December 28, 1976.

18) The Jewish Visual Library, "Chaim Weizmann," www.jewishvirtual library.org/jsource/biography/weizmann.html.

19) Truman. pp. 157-158.

20) Ibid., p. 160.

21) Ibid.

22) McCullough, p. 608.

23) Ibid., p. 609.

24) Robert H. Ferrell, ed., *Off the Record: The Private Papers of Harry S. Truman* (Columbia, MO: University of Missouri Press, 1997), p. 127.

25) McCullough, p. 611.

26) Truman, p. 165.

27) Edward Jacobson, "Two Presidents and a Haberdasher — 1948," *American Jewish Archives*, 1968.

28) McCullough, pp. 614-615.

29) Ibid., p. 616.

30) Ibid,. pp. 617-618.

31) Ibid., p. 620.

32) Alfred Steinberg, *The Man from Missouri: The Life and Times of Harry S. Truman* (New York: Putnam, 1962) p. 308. See also, Merle Miller, *Plain Speaking: An Oral Biography of Harry S. Truman* (New York: Putnam, 1974), pp. 235-236.

33) Sachar, p. 312.

34) Miller, pp. 52, 230-231.

35) McCullough, p. 286.

Chapter 7: Revival of the Language

1) Robert St. John, *The Life Story of Ben-Yehuda: Tongue of the Prophets* (Noble, OK: Balfour Books, 2013), pages 23-26. This book was originally published in 1952. It is based on conversations with Ben-Yehuda's second wife, Hemda, and a biography she wrote about her husband in Hebrew. It is also based on interviews with

friends and scholars who knew Ben-Yehuda personally.

2) Libby Kantorwitz, "Eliezer Ben-Yehuda and the Resurgence of the Hebrew Language," *The Jewish Magazine*, www.jewishmag.com.

3) Malka Drucker, *Eliezer Ben-Yehuda: The Father of Modern Hebrew* (New York: Lodestar Books, 1987), page 6. A brief but very insightful biography, particularly regarding the nature, use and development of the Hebrew language.

4) Eliezer Ben-Yehuda, *Fulfillment of Prophecy: the Life Story of Eliezer Ben-Yehuda 1858-1922* (Privately printed, 2008), page 115. The author is Ben-Yehuda's grandson who has the same name as his grandfather. Based on letters, family remembrances and unpublished autobiographical segments written by Ben-Yehuda about his early life.

5) Ben-Yehuda, page 16.

6) Jack Fellman, "Hebrew: Eliezer Ben-Yehuda & the Revival of Hebrew," www.jewishvirtuallibrary.org, page 5.

7) Barry Rubin, *Assimilation and its Discontents* (New York: Times Books, 1995), page 4.

8) Drucker, page 17.

9) Ben-Yehuda, page 26.

10) St. John, pages 29-35.

11) Ben-Yehuda, pages 19-23.

12) St. John, page 35.

13) Ben-Yehuda, page 28.

14) St. John, page 43.

15) Ibid.

16) St. John, page 44.

17) Ibid., 46.

18) Ben-Yehuda, pages 48-50.

19) Drucker, page 20.

20) Ibid., page 21.

21) Ben-Yehuda, page 51.

22) Ibid.

23) Drucker, page 22.

24) Ben-Yehuda, pages 55-56.

25) Ibid., page 57.

26) Ibid., pages 62-63.

27) Ibid., pages 68-72.

28) Drucker, page 24.

29) Ibid., page 23.

30) Ibid., page 29.

31) Ben-Yehuda, page 82.

32) Ibid., page 94.

33) Drucker, page 28.

34) Ben-Yehuda, pages 111-112.

35) Drucker, page 29.

36) St. John, page 243.

37) Fellman, page 4.

38) St. John, page 87.

39) Ben-Yehuda, page 147.

40) Ibid., page 139.

41) Ibid., pages 146-147.

42) Ibid., page 147.

43) St. John, page 285.

44) Ibid., pages 285 and 287. See also: Fellman, page 3.

45) Ibid., page 288.

46) Ibid., pages 282-283.

47) Ben-Yehuda, pages 114-115.

48) Drucker, pages 56-58; Ben-Yehuda, pages 224-229; and St. John, pages 195-210.

49) St. John, pages 203-204.

50) NSW Board of Jewish Education, "Eliezer Ben-Yehuda," www.bje.org.au, page 1.

51) Ben-Yehuda, page 265.

52) St. John, page 87.

53) Drucker, page 45.

54) Ben-Yehuda, page 198.

55) Ibid., pages 191-192.

56) Ibid., pages 211-212.

57) Ibid., page 205.

58) St. John, page 284.

59) Ben-Yehuda, pages 315-335.

60) Ibid., pages 306-307.

61) Ibid., page 221.

62) St. John, pages 310-311.

63) Drucker, page 67.

64) Yaffah Berlontz, "Hemda Ben-Yehuda," Jewish Women's Archives, www.jwa.org.

65) Drucker, page 71.

66) Ben-Yehuda, page 329.

67) Ibid., page 369.

68) Ibid., pages x-xi.

69) Berlontz, page 29.

70) Jewish Virtual Library, "Academy of the Hebrew Language," www.jewishvirtuallibrary.org.

71) Wikipedia, "Hebrew Language," www.en.wikipedia.org, page 14.

72) Ben-Yehuda, page 219.

73) Jewish Agency for Israel, "Jew! Speak Hebrew!" www.jafi.org, page 2.

74) Ibid., page 3.

75) Ibid.

76) Behadrey Haredim, "Kometz Aleph-Au — How many Hebrew speakers are there in the world?" www.bhol.co.il.

77) Ben-Yehuda, page 373.

Chapter 8: Reclamation of the Land

1) Jewish Virtual Library, "The Kibbutz," www.jewishvirtuallibrary.org/jsource/Society_&_Culture/kibbutz.html.

2) Jewish Federation of Jacksonville, "History of Hadera-Eiron Region." http://jewishjacksonville.org/page.aspx?id=212161.

3) M. G. Wolman and F. G. A. Fournier, editors, *Land Transformation in Agriculture* (Hoboken, NJ: John Wiley & Sons, 1987), chapter 8 by D. H. K. Amiran, "Land Transformation in Israel," page 295.

4) Roy Allan Anderson and Jay Milton Hoffman, *All Eyes on Israel* (Ft. Worth, TX: Harvest Press, Inc., 1975. Revised edition in 1977), page 37.

5) Wolman and Fournier, *Land Transformation in Agriculture*, page 292.

6) Ibid., page 6.

7) Hearings before the Committee on Foreign Affairs of the House of Representatives of the Sixty-Seventh Congress of the United States, "Establishment of a National Home in Palestine," 1922, page 8.

8) Grant Jeffrey, "Revelation in our Generation?" www.theforbiddenknowledge.com/hardtruth/revelation_our_generation.htm. (An excerpt from Jeffrey's book, *The Signature of God* published by Thomas Nelson in 1998.)

9) Jewish National Fund, "Our History," www.jnf.org/about-jnf/history.

10) Wikipedia, "Jewish National Fund," http://en.wikipedia.org/wiki/Jewish_National_Fund, page 2.

11) Ibid.

12) Jewish National Fund, "Our History," page 1.

13) Ibid.

14) Ibid.

15) Wikipedia, "Jewish National Fund," page 2.

16) Jewish National Fund, "Our History," page 4.

17) Anderson and Hoffman, *All Eyes on Israel*, page 35.

18) Jewish National Fund, "Over 240 million trees planted," www.jnf.org/work-we-do/our-projects/forestry-ecology, page 1.

19) Ibid.

20) Wikipedia, "National Water Carrier of Israel," http://en.wikipedia.org/wiki/National_Water_Carrier_of_Israel, page 2.

21) Jon Fedler, "Israeli Agriculture: Coping with Growth," www.jewishvirtuallibrary.org/jsource/agriculture/aggrowth.html, page 3.

22) Rowan Jacobsen, "Israel Proves the Desalination Era Is Here," *Scientific American*, July 29, 2016, www.scientificamerican.com/article/israel-proves-the-desalination-era-is-here, page 3.

23) Ibid., page 4.

24) Ibid.

25) Ben Sales, "Water surplus in Israel? With desalination, once unthinkable is possible," www.jta.org, page 1.

26) Sales, page 2.

27) Dan Lenski, "Is Israel self-sufficient in food production?" www.quora.com/Is-Israel-self-sufficient-in-food-production

28) Wikipedia, "Agriculture in Israel," https://en.wikipedia.org/wiki/Agriculture_in_Israel, page 3. See also: Jon Fedler, "Israeli Agriculture: Coping with Growth," www.jewishvirtuallibrary.org, pages 7-8.

29) Wikipedia, "Agriculture in Israel," pages 3-4, and Fedler, "Israeli Agriculture . . ." page 8.

30) Wikipedia, "Agriculture in Israel," page 4.

31) Ibid.

32) Ibid., page 5. See also: Fedler, "Israeli Agriculture . . ." page 11.

33) Sara Eisen, "Business is blooming for Israeli flowers," www.israel21c.org/business-is-blooming-for-israeli-flowers, page 1.

34) Ibid.

35) Jonathan D. Auerback, "Turning sand into land: Desert farms in Israel grow lush crops from sand and salty water," *The Christian Science Monitor,* May 19, 1987, page 1.

36) Abigail Klein Leichman, "12 top ways Israel feeds the world," May 10, 2012, www.israel21c.org/the-12-ways-israel-feeds-the-world.

37) Auerback, "Turning sand into land . . ." page 3.

38) Ibid.

39) Grant Jeffrey, "Revelation in our Generation?" (See #8 above).

Chapter 9: The Resurgence of the Military

1) *Akhbar el-Yom* newspaper (Egypt), "Interview with Abd al-Rahman Azzam Pasha," October 11, 1947. (Translated by R. Green.) Referenced in "Israeli War of Independence: Background & Overview," Jewish Virtual Library, www.jewishvirtuallibrary.org/jsource/History/1948_War.html, page 3.

2) Golda Meir, *My Life* (NY: Dell, 1975), pp. 213, 222, 224.

3) Benny Morris, *The Road to Jerusalem: Glubb Pasha, Palestine and the Jews* (London: I. B. Tauris, 2003), page 35.

4) Wikipedia, "1948 Arab-Israeli War," http://en.wikipedia.org/wiki/1948_Arab%Ezekiel%93Israeli_War, page 40.

5) Benny Morris, *A History of the First Arab-Israeli War* (New Haven, CT: Yale University Press, 2008). Referenced in Wikipedia, "Battle of Yad Mordechai," http:en.wikipedia.org/wiki/Battle_of_Yad_Mordechai.

6) *Zionism and Israel Encyclopedic Dictionary*, "Battle of Yad Mordechai, 1948," http://zionism-israel.com/dic/Yad_Mordechai_battle.htm, page 1.

7) Ibid., page 4.

8) Ibid., page 5.

9) Samuel Katz, *Battleground — Fact and Fantasy in Palestine* (NY: Bantam Books, 1985), pages 10-11, 185.

10) Netanel Lorch, *One Long War* (Jerusalem: Keter, 1976), page 110.

11) Isi Leibler, *The Case for Israel* (Australia: The Globe Press, 1972) page 18.

12) Leibler, page 60.

13) Ibid., page 18.

14) Ibid., page 60.

15) Ibid., page 18.

16) Chaim Herzog, *The Arab-Israeli Wars* (NY: Random House, 1982), page 149.

17) Jewish Virtual Library, "The Six-Day War: Background & Overview," www.jewishvirtuallibrary.org/jsource/ History/67_War.html,

pages 3-4.

18) Dan Fisher, *The Los Angeles Times*, "The Six Day War 20 Years After," May 31, 1987, page 1.

19) Wikipedia, "Yom Kippur War," http://en.wikipedia.org/wiki/Yom_Kippur_War, page 12.

20) Mitchell Bard, "The 1973 Yom Kippur War," www.jewishvirtuallibrary.org/jsource/History73_War.html, page 2.

21) Bard, page 3.

22) Ibid., pages 5-6.

23) Ido Netanyahu, *Entebbe: A Defining Moment in the War on Terrorism — The Jonathan Netanyahu Story* (Noble, OK: Balfour Books, 2003). A good website dedicated to the life of Yoni Netanyahu and the Entebbe raid can be found at www.yoni.org.il/en. An excellent article about the raid appeared in *Air Force Magazine*, December 2010, vol. 93, no. 12. The article was written by John T. Correll and was titled, "Entebbe." It can be found on the Internet at www.airforcemag.com/MagazineArchive/Pages/2010/December%202010 Entebbe.aspx.

24) Wikipedia, "Operation Entebbe," http://en.wikipedia.org/wiki/OperationEntebbe, page 10.

25) Ibid.

26) Netanyahu, *Entebbe*, page 199.

27) Peter Scott Ford, "Israel's Attack on Osariq: A Model for Future Preventive Strikes?" Master's thesis presented to the Naval Postgraduate School, September 2004. Available on the Internet at www.fas.org/man/eprint/ford.pdf, pages 3,17-20.

28) Moshe Fuksman-Sha'al, *Israel's Strike Against the Iraqi Nuclear Reactor 7 June, 1981 — a Collection of Articles and Lectures,* (Jerusalem: Menachem Begin Heritage Center, 2003 edition). From the chapter by Rafael Eitan entitled, "The Raid on the Reactor from the Point of View of the Chief of Staff."

29) Jewish Virtual Library, "Operation Opera: The Israeli Raid on the Osirak Nuclear Reactor," www.jewishvirtuallibrary.org/jsource/History/Osirak.html, page 6.

30) Moshe Fuksman-Sha'al, chapter by Rafael Eitan.

31) Ibid.

32) Gary Solis, *The Law of Armed Conflict: International Humanitarianism in War* (Cambridge U. Press, 2010), page 182.

33) Avraham Shmuel Lewin, "Osirak Revisited," FrontPage magazine, *The Jewish Press*, December 18, 2007. Available on the Internet at http://archive.frontpagemag.com/readArticle.aspx?ARTID=29258.

Chapter 10: Re-occupation of Jerusalem

1) Sir Robert Anderson, *The Coming Prince* (Grand Rapids, MI: Kregel Classics, 1957). Originally published in 1894.

2) Dan Fisher, "A Region Reshaped by the 6-Day War: The Legacy of Conflict Series: The Six-Day War: 20 Years After," *The Los Angeles Times*, May 31, 1987, page 1.

3) U.S. Department of State, Office of the Historian, "Oil Embargo, 1973–1974," https://history.state.gov/milestones/1969-1976/oil-embargo.

4) Israel Ministry of Foreign Affairs, "Statement to the Knesset by Prime Minister Ben-Gurion." December 5, 1949.

5) Kate Samuelson, "Why Jerusalem Isn't Recognized as Israel's Capital," *Time* magazine, December 16, 2016, http://time.com/4604739/david-friedman-jerusalem-jewish-israel.

6) David B. Green, "This Day in Jewish History 1980: Israel Enacts the Symbolic 'Jerusalem, Capital of Israel' Law," www.haaretz.com/jewish/this-day-in-jewish-history/premium-1.668420.

Chapter 11: Refocusing of World Politics

1) Sharona Schwartz, "The U.N.'s Treatment of Israel Summed Up in One Stunning Graphic," www.theblaze.com/news/2015/06/25/the-u-n-s-treatment-of-israel-summed-up-in-one-stunning-graphic.

2) UN Watch, "Report: In 9 Years' Existence, UNHRC Condemned Israel More Times Than Rest of World Combined," June 25, 2015, www.unwatch.org/report-in-9-years-existence-unhrc-condemned-israel-more-times-than-rest-of-world-combined.

3) Ibid.

4) Ibid.

5) Anne Bayefsky, "The World Against Israel – New UN Report Enables Worldwide Hatred of Israel with Bias Report," www.prophecynewswatch.com/2015/April01/013.html.

6) Pini Dunner, "The UN is an Enemy in Sheep's Clothing," http://prophecynewswatch.com/article.cfm?recent_news_id=231, pages 3-4.

7) *Newsweek* cover, "Exodus: Why Europe's Jews Are Fleeing Once Again," August 8, 2014.

8) *U.S. News & World Report*, "An Unsafe Place for Jews," www.usnews.com/opinion/blogs/world-report/2015/04/02/europe-has-a-problem-with-virulent-anti-semitism, page 1.

9) Ibid.

10) Ibid., page 2.

11) Adam Lebor, "Exodus: Why Europe's Jews Are Fleeing Once Again," www.newsweek.com/2014/08/08/exodus-why-europes-jews-are-fleeing-once-again-261854.html, July 29, 2014, page 2.

12) Michael Lipka, "The Continuing Decline of Europe's Jewish Population," http://www.pewresearch.org/fact-tank/2015/02/09/europes-jewish-population.

13) Matthew Hamilton, "Hanegraaff and Burge Attack Christian Support of Israel," *Juicy Ecumenicism*, July 17, 2012, https://juicyecumenism.com/2012/07/17/hanegraaff-and-burge-attack-christian-support-of-israel.

14) Dennis Prager and Joseph Telushkin, *Why the Jews?: The Reason for Antisemitism* (New York, NY: Touchstone, 2003).

15) James A. Showers, "The New Anti-Semitism," *Israel My Glory* magazine, January-February 2013, p. 15.

16) Jacob Prasch, "Stephen Sizer and the Sons of Menelaus," www.moriel.org/component/k2/item/317-stephen-sizer-and-the-sons-of-menelaus.html?ml=1, page 1.

17) Andrew D. Robinson, "The Error of Replacement Theology - Part 1," www.cwm.org.au/3/23-64/56-7, page 4.

18) Justin Cohen, "'Show me evidence Israel wasn't behind 9/11', asks vicar Stephen Sizer," *Jewish News Online,* January 29, 2015.

19) Bishop Andrew Watson, "Statement on the Reverend Stephen Sizer by the Bishop of Guildford," February 9, 2015, www.cofeguildford.org.uk/whats-on/news/detail/2015/02/09/statement-on-the-revd-stephen-sizer-by-the-bishop-of-guildford.

20) World Council of Churches, "Kairos Palestine Document," section 2.5, www.oikoumene.org/en/resources/documents/other-ecumenical-bodies/kairos-palestine-document.

21) T.A. McMahon, "Chrislam? Christian Palestinianism?" *The Berean Call*, January 1, 2012, www.thebereancall.org/content/chrislam-christian-palestinianism-1, page 3.

22) Ibid., page 3.

23) Alan Hart, "The New Nazis," January 13, 2009, www.alanhart.net/the-new-nazis.

24) David Bukay, "Peace or Jihad? Abrogation in Islam," *The Middle East Quarterly*, Fall 2007, Volume 14, Number 4, www.meforum.org/1754/peace-or-jihad-abrogation-in-islam, pages 3-11.

25) WikiIslam, "List of Abrogations in the Qur'an," https://wikiislam.net/wiki/List_of_Abrogations_in_the_Qur'an.

26) Martin Luther, "On the Jews and Their Lies," 1543, http://vho.org/aaargh/fran/livres9/Luthereng.pdf.

27) Wikipedia, "Antisemitism in Japan," https://en.wikipedia.org/wiki/Antisemitism_in_Japan.

28) For detailed information about President Truman's recognition of Israel, see "Israel's 60th Anniversary," by Dr. David R. Reagan, *Lamplighter* magazine, March-April 2008, pages 3-9.

29) Shlomo Slonim, "The 1948 American Embargo on Arms to Israel," *Political Science Quarterly,* Vol. 94, No. 3, Autumn, 1979, pages 495ff.

30) Jewish Virtual Library, "The Sinai-Suez Campaign: President Eisenhower & PM Ben-Gurion on Israeli Withdrawal from Sinai," www.jewishvirtuallibrary.org/jsource/US-Israel/phantom.html.

31) Donald Neff, "How Eisenhower Forced Israel to End Occupation After Sinai Crisis: When an American President Said No to Israel," Institute for Historical Review, www.ihr.org/jhr/v16/v16n2p14Neff.html, page 2.

32) John F. Kennedy, "Speech by Senator John F. Kennedy, Zionists of America Convention, Statler Hilton Hotel, New York, NY, August 26, 1960," www.presidency.ucsb.edu/ws/?pid=74217.

33) Ibid.

34) Stephen M. Walt, *The Origins of Alliances*, (Ithaca, NY: Cornell University Press, 1987) pp. 95-96.

35) Morris Smith, "Our First Jewish President Lyndon Johnson?" *5 Towns Jewish Times*, http://5tjt.com/our-first-jewish-president-lyndon-johnson-an-update.

36) Ibid.

37) Jim Byron, "How Richard Nixon Saved Israel," http://blog.nixon foundation.org/2010/10/how-richard-nixon-saved-israel, page 1.

38) *Haaretz*, "Gerald Ford, the U.S. president who reassessed policy toward Israel, dies at 93," December 28, 2006, page 2.

39) Christa Case Bryant, "Netanyahu-Obama tensions nothing new: 5 low points in US-Israel ties," *Christian Science Monitor*, September 27, 2012, www.unitedjerusalem.org/ndex2.aspid=1612216&Date= 10/17/2012, page 2.

40) Bernard Gwertzman, "Egypt and Israel Sign Formal Treaty, Ending a State of War After 30 Years; Sadat and Begin Praise Carter's Role," *The New York Times*, March 26, 1979.

41) Jimmy Carter, *Palestine: Peace Not Apartheid* (New York, NY: Simon & Schuster, 2006).

42) Jewish Virtual Library, "The Reagan Plan," www.jewishvirtual library.org/jsource/Peace/reaganplan.html, page 3.

43) Chemi Shalev, "If Obama treated Israel like Reagan did, he'd be impeached," *Haaretz*, December 9, 2011, www.haaretz.com/blogs/ west-of-eden/if-obama-treated-israel-like-reagan-did-he-d-be-imp eached-1.400542.

44) Mitchell Bard, "Reagan's Legacy on Israel," www.mitchellbard. com/articles/reagan.html, page 1.

45) Ibid., page 1.

46) Ibid.

47) U.S. Department of State, Office of the Historian, "The Reagan Administration and Lebanon, 1981–1984," https://history.state.gov/ milestones/1981-1988/lebanon, page 2.

48) Mitchell Bard, "Reagan's Legacy on Israel," page 2.

49) Foundation for Middle East Peace, "U.S. Policy on Jerusalem," www.fmep.org/reports/special-reports/special-report-jerusalem/ u.s.-policy-on-jerusalem.

50) U.S. Department of State, Office of the Historian, "The Madrid Conference, 1991," http://history.state.gov/milestones/1989-1992 madrid-conference, page 2.

51) Sheryl Gay Stolberg, "Bush and Israel: Unlike his father," www. nytimes.com/2006/08/02/world/americas/02iht-bush.2363483.htm

l?page wanted=all&_r=0, page 1.

52) U.S. Department of State, Office of the Historian, "The Oslo Accords and the Arab-Israeli Peace Process," https://history.state.gov/milestones/1993-2000/oslo.

53) Gale Student Resources in Context, 2011, "Bill Clinton's role in Israeli-Palestinian Peace Accords," http://ic.galegroup.com/ic/suic/ReferenceDetailsPage, page 2.

54) *Time* magazine, "Sixteen Years of Israeli-Palestinian Summits: Wye River Summit," http://content.time.com/time/specials/2007/article/0,28804,1644149_1644147_1644132,00.html.

55) Jewish Virtual Library, "2000 Camp David Summit: Background & Overview" by David Shyovitz, www.jewishvirtuallibrary.org/jsource/Peace/cd2000art.html.

56) Sheryl Gay Stolberg, (see #51 above).

57) The White House, "President Bush's Freedom Agenda Helped Protect The American People," http://georgewbush-whitehouse.archives.gov/infocus/bushrecord/factsheets/freedomagenda.html, page 1.

58) Joel Brinkley and Steven R. Weisman, "Rice Urges Israel and Palestinians to Sustain Momentum," www.nytimes.com/2005/08/18/international/middleeast/18rice.html, page 1.

59) Al Arabiya News, "Obama tells Al Arabiya peace talks should resume," www.alarabiya.net/articles/2009/01/27/65087.html.

60) The White House, "Remarks by the President on a New Beginning, Cairo University, June 4, 2009," www.whitehouse.gov/ the_press_office/remarks-by-the-President-at-Cairo-University-6-04-09.

61) Seth Mandel, "Contentions On Israel, Obama Discovers the Obvious," *Commentary* magazine, November 21, 2012, www.commentarymagazine.com/2012/11/21/on-israel-obama-discovers-the-obvious.

62) Michael Reagan, "Israeli Prime Minister Mistreated by Obama," *Patriot Update*, May 19, 2011, http://patriotupdate.com/articles/israeli-prime-minister-mistreated-by-obama.

63) Adrian Blomfield, "Obama snubbed Netanyahu for dinner with Michelle and the girls, Israelis claim," *The Telegraph*, March 25, 2010, www.telegraph.co.uk/news/worldnews/barackobama/7521220/ Obama-snubbed-Netanyahu-for-dinner-with-Michelle-and-the-girls-Israelis-claim.html.

64) Tom Cohen, "Obama calls for Israel's return to pre-1967 borders," CNN, May 19, 2011, www.cnn.com/2011/POLITICS/05/19/obama.israel.palestinians.

65) Joel B. Pollak, "State Dept.: Palestinians Do Not Need to Recognize Israel as Jewish State," www.breitbart.com/Big-Peace/2014/03/09/State-Dept-Palestinians-Do-Not-Need-to-Recognize-Israel-as-Jew ish-State.

66) Ynet News, "Obama says settlement building illegitimate," September 23, 2009, www.ynetnews.com/articles/0,7340,L-3781 005, 00.html.

67) Congressional Research Service, "U.S. Foreign Aid to the Palestinians," by Jim Zanotti, September 30, 2013, Summary page (no page number), www.fas.org/sgp/crs/mideast/RS22967.pdf.

68) Joel Brinkley and Steven R. Weisman, "Rice Urges Israel and Palestinians to Sustain Momentum," www.nytimes.com/2005/08/18/international/middleeast/18rice.html, page 1.

69) Congressional Research Service, "U.S. Aid to Israel," by Jeremy M. Sharp, April 11, 2014, summary page (no page number), http://fas.org/sgp/crs/mideast/RL33222.pdf.

70) Peter Baker and Somini Sengupta, "Trump Pressures Obama Over U.N. Resolution on Israeli Settlements,"*The New York Times*, December 22, 2016, www.nytimes.com/2016/12/22/world/middle east/donald-trump-united-nations-israel-settlements.html?_r=0.

71) Amir Tibon, Report: "Trump Will Not Move U.S. Embassy to Jerusalem Quickly," *Haaretz*, January 23, 2017, www.haaretz.com /israel-news/1.766964.

72) Carlos Garcia, "Trump comes out against Israeli settlements," *The Blaze News*, February 2, 2017, www.theblaze.com/news/2017/02/02/breaking-trump-comes-out-against-israeli-settlements.

73) Michael Wilner, "Trump: Jared Kushner Will 'Broker Mideast Peace' For the White House," *The Jerusalem Post*, January 16, 2017, www.jpost.com/American-Politics/Jared-Kushner-will- broker -Middle-East-peace-at-the-White-House-says-Trump-478554.

74) Colin Dwyer, "Paris Summit Urges Two-State Solution To Israeli-Palestinian Conflict," *NPR News*, January 15, 2017, www.npr.org/sections/thetwo-way/2017/01/15/509939635/dozens-of-diplo mats-gather-in-paris-for-israel-palestinian-peace-talks.

75) *BrainyQuote*, "Winston Churchill," www.brainyquote.com/quotes/quotes/w/winstonchu100130.html.

Chapter 12: The Redemption of Israel

1) Bill Salus, *Isralestine* (Crane, MO: HighWay, a division of Anomalos Publishing House, 2008).

2) Ron Rhodes, *North Storm Rising* (Eugene, OR: Harvest House, 2008).

About the Author

Dr. David R. Reagan is the Senior Evangelist for Lamb & Lion Ministries, a Bible prophecy ministry located in the Dallas, Texas area.

Before founding the ministry in 1980, Dr. Reagan served for 20 years as a university professor, teaching international law and politics. Throughout that time he was an ardent student of the Bible. All his advanced degrees were earned at The Fletcher School of Law & Diplomacy, a graduate school of international relations in the Boston area that is owned and operated jointly by Tufts and Harvard Universities.

Since 1980 Dr. Reagan has taught Bible prophecy in meetings and seminars held all across America and around the world. His weekly television program, "Christ in Prophecy," is broadcast both nationally and internationally.

He has led over 45 pilgrimages to Israel and is considered to be an expert on Middle East politics and Israel in Bible prophecy.

Dr. Reagan has been gifted with the skill to communicate complex ideas in simple, understandable terms. He is the author of 14 books, including one of the only children's books ever published about end time Bible prophecy. It is titled *Jesus Is Coming Again!*

Dr. Reagan and his wife, Ann, have been married more than 55 years. They live in a suburb of Dallas, Texas. They are the parents of two daughters and have four grandchildren and two great grandsons.

You can find more detailed information about every aspect of Lamb & Lion Ministries at the ministry's website: www.lamblion.com.

Dr. Reagan's Commentary on the Book of Revelation

This book provides a sweeping overview of the book of Revelation, examining it in detail chapter-by-chapter.

The book begins by laying down guidelines for the interpretation of Bible prophecy, insisting that it be interpreted for its plain sense meaning. Then, using those guidelines, Dr. Reagan takes the reader through the book of Revelation, explaining each chapter in detail. He then shows how to systematize the book into a comprehensive sequence of events. He then shifts his focus to the most commonly asked questions about the book, supplying the reader with biblically based answers. The book concludes with Dr. Reagan showing the reader how to apply the message of Revelation to the challenge of Christian living today. The specific chapters are as follows:

- Understanding Revelation
- Interpreting Revelation
- Systematizing Revelation
- Probing Revelation
- Applying Revelation

This is an easy to understand book for the layman. It is designed to clear away the mystery of Revelation, showing what it means about the future while making it relevant to daily living in the present. The book contains many helpful charts and diagrams. It also has an annotated bibliography of resources pertaining to the book of Revelation. 263 pages. $20 including the cost of shipping.

This book has been translated and published in more than a dozen languages throughout the world.

You can order a copy by calling 972-736-3567, Monday through Friday, 8am to 5pm Central time. You can also purchase the book through the Lamb & Lion website at www.lamblion.com.

Dr. Reagan's In-Depth Study of the Signs of the Times

An exhaustive study of the signs of the times that clearly indicate that we are living in the season of the Lord's return. Contains an overview of all the signs plus chapters on each of the nine major signs.

A very unique feature of the book is that it contains a prophetic forum in which 22 Bible prophecy experts respond to 11 questions about the signs of the times.

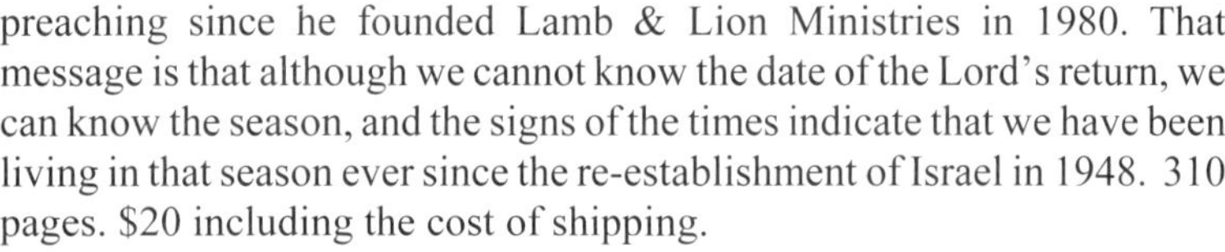

This book features the basic message that Dr. Reagan has been preaching since he founded Lamb & Lion Ministries in 1980. That message is that although we cannot know the date of the Lord's return, we can know the season, and the signs of the times indicate that we have been living in that season ever since the re-establishment of Israel in 1948. 310 pages. $20 including the cost of shipping.

You can order a copy by calling 972-736-3567, Monday through Friday, 8am to 5pm Central time. You can also purchase the book through the Lamb & Lion website at www.lamblion.com.

The Lamb & Lion Television Program

Lamb & Lion Ministries produces a weekly television program called "Christ in Prophecy" that is broadcast both nationally and internationally. It is designed to teach the fundamentals of Bible prophecy and to alert people to the soon return of Jesus.

You can find the program on most of the national Christian television networks, and you can also watch it on demand at the ministry's website at www.lamblion.com.

Dr. Reagan's Refutation of Heresies Concerning the Jewish People

This book focuses on the evil of Replacement Theology and the tragedy of Dual Covenant Theology. In the process, it deals with the following questions, among others:

- Have the Jews ceased to be God's Chosen People?
- Are they guilty of the unforgivable sin of "killing God."?
- Has God replaced them with the Church?
- Has God transferred their promises to the Church?
- Have they lost all hope as a nation?
- Are they devoid of any role in the end times?
- If God still loves them, how could He allow them to experience the Holocaust?
- Do they have their own way of salvation, separate and apart from Jesus?

Other topics covered in the book include the phenomenon of Messianic Judaism, the hope of Christian Zionism, the horror of the Holocaust, and the most important prophetic development of the 20th Century. Dr. Reagan also takes a look at the Middle East crisis in biblical perspective.

The books runs 232 pages in length and sells for $20, including the cost of shipping.

You can order it via our website at www.lamblion. com. Or, you can call us at 972-736-3567 Monday through Friday, 8am to 5pm Central Time.

intermediate body

JGL ?